High praise for
The Divorce Recovery Journal ...

"The Divorce Recovery Journal offers empathy and hope through the painful time of separation and divorce. It reminds us that we are never truly alone, and that at the darkest moments, when all seems lost, a way lies waiting for us, a path hewn from the pain and suffering of those who have gone before us. The Divorce Recovery Journal shows a deep understanding of healing; it draws on what is common to divorce, but encourages readers to find their own way to acceptance and peace." ***Daniel C. Frigo, Ph.D.***

"... an excellent resource for someone in the throes of a divorce ... also a useful tool for divorce support groups ... the selected quotes and thoughts are witty and engaging, sometimes funny, sometimes poignant ... this book could easily become a good and trusted friend." ***The Reverend Janet Pillman***

"When I set sail on the emotional sea of divorce, I was advised by my therapist, my recovery group, my attorney, and my friends to journal my way through it. Many times my mind was too full, too empty, too confused to sort through or focus my thoughts, and I would end up with a meandering stream of consciousness that only confirmed my unrest and my confusion. The Divorce Recovery Journal became an important tool in this process. It helped me to focus on pertinent issues and put some order in my life at a time when upheaval was a daily challenge." ***Lana Hagan***

"This journal is a great tool for structuring your internal healing when you're going through the divorce process. I plan to recommend it to all my divorcing clients."
Mary Meidinger, M.Ed., Licensed Professional Counselor

"Now in addition to our hard work and advice, we attorneys and mediators can offer our clients another genuinely helpful resource – The Divorce Recovery Journal – we can even assign pages in the Journal as homework. With its blend of serious and humorous words and lots of open space, this book is a valuable tool in dealing with the divorce process. Thank you, Senn and Stuart."

Timothy Gardner, Attorney and Divorce Mediator

"I went through a divorce after 29 years of marriage. If there had been a journal like this available to help me through the process at that time, I know it would have made things easier. Knowing others have been there and not only survived, but have actually grown spiritually, learning (or re-learning) the value of autonomy, is both comforting and validating." *Judy Highfill*

"This book is filled with 'hard won' wisdom. Its format facilitates healthy self reflection and 'here and now' moments."

Ralph Orlovick, Ph.D., psychologist
author of Sobriety Jungle: Which path will you choose?

THE
DIVORCE
RECOVERY
JOURNAL

*by **Linda C. Senn** and **Mary Stuart**, M.A.*

PEN
CENTRAL
PRESS

Other books by Linda C. Senn:

Your Pocket Divorce Guide

10 Effective Ways to Promote Your Seminar

"The Divorce Recovery Journal"
by Linda C. Senn and Mary Stuart, M.A.

Published by: PEN CENTRAL PRESS
Division of Pen Central Communications
P. O. Box 220369
St. Louis MO 63122-0369

Graphic art by Bellm Graphics
Printed by BookMasters, Inc., Mansfield, Ohio 44905

Copyright © 1999 Linda C. Senn and Mary Stuart

ISBN 0-9665672-2-6

ACKNOWLEDGMENTS

Mary and Linda would like to acknowledge their three
ex-husbands without whom this book
would not have been possible.

In regard to our own personal growth we would both like
to thank our most excellent therapists who assisted us along
our paths to recovery.

We also want to thank Marla Niemeir, Pamela Picker
and Mel Jernigan for their thoughtful input.

4

TABLE OF CONTENTS

Foreword

Divorce is a highly stressful and emotional life event, particularly in the acute phase during which you need the love and support of friends and family for a healthy recovery. Even after progressing through that phase, many people discover that every so often they have an attack of the "acutes" and need someone to talk to.

Divorce is also a period of intense self-examination. It has the potential for either personal growth or personal shrinking, depending upon how you handle the process.

The Divorce Recovery Journal will help in both those areas. It will be your best friend in the wee hours of the morning when you need someone to help you make it through the night. Its thought-provoking messages and guides to introspection lead you through the maze of emotional turmoil to self-awareness, understanding, acceptance and forgiveness. It helps you heal your heart and spirit so you can successfully move into the next step in your life plan.

And for those filled with anger and the thirst for revenge, just think of it this way: the sweetest revenge you can have is to be happy, well-adjusted, and successful after your divorce. The Divorce Recovery Journal can help you achieve that.

The insights Mary and Linda have gained in their journeys through divorce can be enormously helpful and comforting to those who are traveling that path themselves. Let them take your hand and lead you through the chaos to a healthy recovery.

Laura Johnson,
author of Divorce Strategy:
Tactics for a Civil Financial Divorce

Introduction

When we went through the divorce process ourselves, we searched to no avail for a book like this one with its healing advice and insights. This book was born out of our frustration at not finding it, or anything like it. With so much to learn and unlearn at the same time, the process can overwhelm even the most capable, stretching our meager energy reserves almost to the snapping point. What was needed, we felt, was a sort of instruction manual to help people through the long transition, to help the healing that's required after such a blow to the body, mind and spirit.

The Divorce Recovery Journal is divided into three phases: looking down, looking out and looking up. The first phase, *Looking Down*, represents the time when you can scarcely lift your head out of the black hole of desolation. The second, *Looking Out*, deals with the divorce itself and offers some effective coping mechanisms for getting through it with the least amount of damage. *Looking Up* moves you along into the new life of real recovery. These sections cover the roller coaster time from separation through the divorce to a reasonably balanced new life.

The book contains frequent splashes of humor. We know humor can feel foreign and even awkward in these turbulent times, but it's a great healing agent, and we encourage you to join in the healthy act of laughing as often and heartily as possible. It will help you keep your perspective through the chaos.

We hope that you, the reader, will benefit from those who have trod this path before you. One of the most beneficial exercises you can do while enduring an emotional trauma is to journal your thoughts and feelings. Therefore, we have left space on each page for you to jot down your entries ...written or pictorial. It's our belief that you can never express yourself too much, so consider expanding your entries into a full-size journal.

Read the book from beginning to end, then go back and reread the pages of each phase when you feel it applies to your situation. If you write your journal notes as you go, you'll gain empowering insights into your own growth as an individual. From time to time go back and make later entries below your original ones. One month or three can make a big difference in your outlook.

Take this book with you when you get together with other divorced or divorcing friends and use its pages as springboards for discussion. You can learn a lot from others' experiences and philosophies.

The advice you read between the covers of this book has been gleaned from personal experience, interviews, research, seminar presentations, and in Mary's case, from years of counseling others through these major life transitions.

By the way, many readers have asked who **Venus Veritas** is. Venus is the combined alter ego of Linda and Mary ... in other words, Venus 'R' Us. And she can be a very insightful creature.

Now in the spirit of those who have experienced this event before you, we wish you thoughtful, meaningful reading and writing.

PHASE I

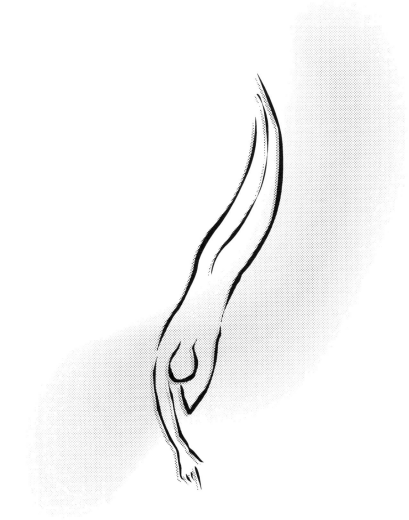

LOOKING DOWN

Life's under no obligation to give us
what we expect.
~ Margaret Mitchell

Our Thoughts:
It's desirable to have expectations, wants and goals. We all have
them, and it's a normal human condition to dream. But if we
begin to believe we're entitled, life has a way of reminding us
that we can be wrong. Approach life with open hands, open heart
… and open expectations.

Your Thoughts:
Do I feel entitled?

The only cure for seasickness is
to sit on the shady side of an
old brick church in the country.
~ English sailors' proverb

Our Thoughts:

Divorce can be nauseating, just like seasickness. The point to this proverb is to avoid the irritant when you think you're going to throw up (either literally or figuratively). Find some place, either internally or externally, where you can be peaceful. Slow down, take a time out, get your land legs back under you.

Your Thoughts:

What are my major irritants?

❧

Journaling is an effective, cheap
way to deal with the scariness and
insecurities of your new single life.
~ Venus Veritas

Our Thoughts:

Journal for the first few weeks of your separation after prying eyes
can no longer invade the privacy of your written thoughts. Don't
make a "should" out of it – just pick up a pen or a keyboard, and
record your feelings, actions, moments of growth and despair,
euphoria and fear. When you read back over your entries in three
months, or six months, or whenever, you'll be gratified to see how
very well you handled the challenges of divorce and starting over.
You may be in awe of the amazingly strong person who dealt with
all that chaos – *you!*

Your Thoughts:

Building on the word "single," what other stream-of-conscious
words bubble up in my mind?

❦

If at first you don't succeed
you're running about average.
~ M. H. Alderson

Our Thoughts:

Oh, how human it is to want to rush personal growth! There is much to be unlearned and relearned right now, and you need to cut yourself some slack. In the early days of separation, you'll have a tough time even understanding the questions, much less working out brilliant answers. Try to be as patient with yourself as you would have others be with you.

Your Thoughts:

How have I been unfairly impatient with myself lately?

❧

One, two, three,
Buckle my shoe.
~ Robert Benchley

Our Thoughts:

Other people don't warn you about how crazy-making extreme stress can be. Be forewarned! The emotional heaves of divorce will leave you feeling brain dead more often than not, and that can be scary. It helps to remember that what you're experience-ing is a "normal" part of the process, and you aren't losing your mind – at least not permanently.

Your Thoughts:

If I were swapping "losing my mind" stories with other divorced people, which stories would I include?

❧

Announcing a break up is awkward at best.
~ Venus Veritas

Our Thoughts:

It may be awkward, but it's a necessary part of recovery. Not only do you need the support of friends, family, and colleagues, but you don't want people sending their "love to the hubby (or wifey)" when your soon-to-be-ex is in Bimini with a new Significant Other. Close friends and family would appreciate a brief phone call when you can manage it. For those you see less often, a note sent either on its own or included in a holiday card can accomplish the same purpose. You aren't asking for a response, just letting others know that you're starting a new life.

Your Thoughts:

Who do I need to contact?

❦

The impossible
is often the untried.
~ Jim Goodwin

Our Thoughts:

Life often feels overwhelming during divorce. Everything looms large and many tasks seem impossible, particularly if this is the first time you've ever done them. If you're feeling swamped, get help. If you've never balanced a checkbook, have someone teach you how. If you've never taken the car to the mechanic, take a friend with you who has had experience in dealing with mechanics. Reach out and ask for help. You'll be amazed at the response.

Your Thoughts:

What prevents me from asking for help?

❧

Being alone is a markedly different
experience than being lonely.
~ La Rochefoucaud

Our Thoughts:

Being alone can be a singularly pleasurable experience. You can be quiet, enjoying the silence or you can make a joyful noise only your ears hear. You can do whatever you please, including nothing at all. Loneliness is another state altogether. It's all about fear, sadness and neediness. We've all been lonely at times, but if you find yourself in the trough of despair too long, think about seeking help.

Your Thoughts:

When do I feel lonely? When do I feel alone?

When a fellow says, "It ain't the money
but the principle of the thing," it's the money.
~ Frank McKinney "Kin" Hubbard

Our Thoughts:

Avoiding confrontation over the property settlement could have
a major impact on your financial future. With so much hurt and
anger present during divorce, it's tempting to say "just take it ...
I don't have any more fight left in me." Weigh your attorney's
advice and your own instincts against your future economic
stability. In most states you can't go back and renegotiate a
property settlement.

Your Thoughts:

How can I keep myself from being emotional about financial
matters in the divorce process?

Think wrongly, if you please, but in all cases
think for yourself.
~ Doris Lessing

Our Thoughts:

When going through a divorce, advice abounds. Friends, professionals, religious figures, children, even your soon-to-be-ex...all have something to say about how you should conduct yourself. Go within and find the place that *knows* what you want. Listen to everyone's input...then decide for yourself.

Your Thoughts:

How good am I at filtering input?

❂

All experience
is an arch to build up.
~ Henry Brooks Adams

Our Thoughts:

"You'll be a better person for it." "You needed this experience to
be the person you've become." Etc. Just when you think you'll
throw up if you hear another well-meaning friend utter one more
platitude, remember this: they're right. No matter how deep your
pain, as humans we *are* the sum of our experiences. Divorce is
but another experience. You'll survive. Really.

Your Thoughts:

How can I survive?

❦

Trust in Allah, but tie your camel.
~ Arabian proverb

Our Thoughts:

You've read in other places in this book that you can't control
everything in your life, and you can't. But during a divorce, you
must plan because in many cases the quality of the rest of your life
depends on it. Don't be a Pollyanna and assume your soon-to-be-
ex will treat you right. You don't have to make him or her into the
devil incarnate, but you do have to be mature and look at the issues
realistically. Know what you want and stick to your guns as much
as you, or the law, will allow.

Your Thoughts:

What are my "camels"?

●

The essence of true friendship
is to make allowance for another's little lapses.
~ David Storey

Our Thoughts:

This cuts two ways. Some friends will inadvertently step on your
toes during the upheaval of your life. They may say "snap out of
it" or blast you with other unfeeling sentiments. Likewise, you
may be fairly inconsiderate due to feeling frazzled and fragmented.
A little flexibility on everyone's part goes a long way toward
keeping treasured friendships.

Your Thoughts:

How gracious am I around friends who may not understand my
pain?

The only thing I regret about my past life is the length
of it. If I had my past life to do over again,
I'd make all the same mistakes—only sooner.
~ Tallulah Bankhead

Our Thoughts:

When divorcing, mistakes made are uppermost in our minds.
It's all too easy to play "if only" games…if only I hadn't done
this or that, maybe it would have worked out. We learn from
our mistakes, and painful as that may be at times, it makes us
who we are.

Your Thoughts:

What are my mistakes teaching me?

True success is overcoming
the fear of being unsuccessful.
~ Paul Sweeney

Our Thoughts:

Practice saying affirmations (positive statements) to yourself –
and do it with conviction. Affirming the natural strength of your
heart, mind, and body and the goodness of your spirit is a fine
way to put the sparkle back in your attitude.

Your Thoughts:

What is my affirmation for today?

❂

> Even if you're on the right track,
> you'll get run over
> if you just sit there.
> ~ Will Rogers

Our Thoughts:

If you're in the immediate aftermath of the nuclear meltdown of your marriage, "just sitting there" is probably all you feel able to do. But eventually, you'll have to pick yourself up and move on before the train called "divorce" squashes you. If you're having trouble moving, get help. Professional help. Help from friends. Help from your priest, rabbi or minister. Whatever. Just get help. You don't have to do this alone.

Your Thoughts:

How can I avoid being run over by the train?

A new relationship is not a life preserver to be clutched at
in lieu of trusting one's own buoyancy.
~ Venus Veritas

Our Thoughts:

It's common for a divorcing person to frantically grasp for a new
relationship as one would grab for a life preserver. But for a
healthy relationship to develop – either friend or lover – it must
be allowed to mature slowly. Clinging to a new Other is far more
likely to strangle it to death than to nurture lovely future possibilities. Take your time.

Your Thoughts:

In what ways am I inclined to cling too much?

❧

Nobody has ever measured, even poets,
how much the heart can hold.
~ Zelda Fitzgerald

Our Thoughts:

You may feel as if your heart is breaking and can't hold one more
painful experience. But it can, and it will. And it will get better
as time goes on. Trust in your resilience. Trust in your Self.
And know that the same heart that is breaking today will be filled
with joy, if not tomorrow, sometime soon.

Your Thoughts:

How resilient am I?

Some mornings it just doesn't seem worth it
to gnaw through the leather straps.
~ Emo Phillips

Our Thoughts:

There are days, weeks even, when you will feel like this. Or perhaps you're in one of those phases right now. You feel crazy, cracked, numb, nuts, bonkers. If people really knew what was going on inside your head, they'd most assuredly lock you up! This is the time to chill out, kick back and do something *extremely* relaxing... something just for you.

Your Thoughts:

How am I feeling crazy?

☯

What you eat standing up doesn't count.
~ Beth Barnes

Our Thoughts:

The newly single are often at a loss when it comes to meals. Many seem to find themselves gulping a can of something over the kitchen sink because cooking and actually sitting down seem like too much effort. *Take the trouble!* Otherwise, you become an uncivilized slob. You're worth the effort.

Your Thoughts:

What are my current eating habits?

❧

I have a simple philosophy.
Fill what's empty. Empty what's full.
Scratch where it itches.
~ Alice Roosevelt Longworth

Our Thoughts:

Take a look at your life. If there are holes deeper than empty space, decide what should go into them. If your calendar or dance card keeps you hopping until you're exhausted, cut something out. Do you have an itch to do something different? Scratch it!

Your Thoughts:

Where am I empty, full and itchy?

❧

No one can make you feel inferior
without your consent.
~ Eleanor Roosevelt

Our Thoughts:

There are times during a divorce when you'll feel less than human,
lower than a snake's belly. Perhaps your spouse or children are
contributing to making you feel like this. Take Eleanor's advice
… don't give your consent.

Your Thoughts:

Am I allowing those around me to put me down?

Nothing in life is to be feared. It is only to be understood.
~ Marie Curie

Our Thoughts:
The very thought of starting a new life alone strikes fear into the
heart of the most capable. In the course of your married life most
decisions and actions were shared – at least theoretically. Now
you have sole responsibility for your life, and possibly that of
your children. However, once you face fear and analyze it, it
usually becomes manageable.

Your Thoughts:
What are my biggest fears?

☯

Welcome
Candlelight flickers
In cut-crystal dishes.
Petite coral rose buds blossom
Fragrant.
~ Linda C. Senn

Our Thoughts:

Whether you're physically moving to a new building or not, your
single home will be your "new home." Think of it as a sanctuary
and fill it with comfort items. Make a list of those things that give
you a lift, perhaps books, photographs, flowers, a favorite old
baseball, incense, wind chimes – and surround yourself with them.

Your Thoughts:

What are some of my favorite comfort items?

☯

Nothing Lasts.
~ Sheldon Kopp

Our Thoughts:

When we marry, we take vows that speak of "until death" and
"forever". Some couples manage to do just that, but since you're
reading this book you probably aren't one of them. You may be
experiencing a broad spectrum of feelings that range all the way
from despair to deranged anger, each of them directed at the
question "Why *didn't* it last?". Even if you're relieved to be out
of the relationship, this question has surely occurred to you.
Well…things change, nothing lasts, and all that jazz. It's true.
Even marriages that endure don't endure in their original states.
Learn to go with the flow of change.

Your Thoughts:

What can I do to help myself deal with change?

The hero is no braver than the ordinary man,
but he is brave five minutes longer.
~ Ralph Waldo Emerson

Our Thoughts:

It takes guts to get through a divorce. There is suffering all
around: the other spouse, children, friends, and you. That any
of us survive is a miracle, but survive we do. And sometimes,
just surviving is all you'll be capable of doing on any given day.
Give yourself those brave five minutes longer.

Your Thoughts:

What are some survival tactics to help me make that five minutes?

☯

> The cure for anything is saltwater—
> sweat, tears, or the sea.
> ~ Isak Dinesen

Our Thoughts:

Just when you think you can't stand feeling miserable one more minute and tears start to flow, an amazing thing happens: after the crying is done you feel better. Not only is it an emotional catharsis, the very act of crying releases certain "feel-good" endorphins into your system that act as natural anti-depressants. Physical activity does the same thing, and the more you sweat, the better you may feel. The sea speaks for itself…there is nothing so calming as being around water. So cry, sweat, and take a cruise!

Your Thoughts:

What is my saltwater "score"?

❧

Sometimes the secret of happiness
involves breaking things.
~ Venus Veritas

Our Thoughts:

Have you ever felt so furious and/or frustrated that you wanted to
smash every dish in the place? Most of us don't indulge in that
fantasy because (1) it would be costly to replace the stuff, and (2)
you would have to clean up the mess when you were through.
There is, however, an ecologically and psychologically helpful
way to get the same release. Take all your breakable trash to the
recycling center, and curse as you hurl every bottle into the pile.
It's a safe way to vent that yen to smash things.

Your Thoughts:

Who can I get to save their empty bottles for me so I'll have more
to smash?

❧

To escape criticism—
do nothing, say nothing, be nothing.
~ Elbert Hubbard

Our Thoughts:

Too many people, influenced by our culture, are inoculated from
birth with conciliation, passivity, and conflict avoidance. You're
in a divorce process…you *must* be assertive when it comes to your
rights. It doesn't matter whether or not your spouse approves any
more, no matter what your history has been. You don't have to be
nasty to be assertive. You don't have to be aggressive. Do what's
right for you.

Your Thoughts:

What is the difference to me between aggressive and assertive?

❧

Everyday living requires courage if life
is to be effective and bring happiness.
~ Maxwell Maltz

Our Thoughts:

This is a time that requires great courage on your part. Whether you are the person leaving the marriage or the one who is left, it takes grit to act and continue living. There is meaning to your life, count on it. Take heart.

Your Thoughts:

What can I do to keep moving?

I never think of the future.
It comes soon enough.
~ Albert Einstein

Our Thoughts:

When the brain is temporarily numb, planning for the future seems overwhelming – just thinking about it makes you want to go take a nap! At those times, live in the moment. Don't plan. Don't anticipate. Don't worry about which bridge to cross and which to burn, just be in the now. It's a lovely rest from all that planning and logic.

Your Thoughts:

What shall I do today *instead* of planning?

❧

I told my mother-in-law that my house was her house,
and she said, "Get the hell off my property."
~ Joan Rivers

Our Thoughts:

Ah, the in-laws. They don't go away just because you and your
spouse divorce. Sometimes you'll remain friends with them,
sometimes not. After the split, they'll remain much as they always
were. Don't ignore them and hope they'll go away, or think they'll
still treat you the same as before. Come to some understanding
with them as to how your relationship will evolve.

Your Thoughts:

What do I feel about my in-laws?

❧

I think somehow we learn who we really are
and then live with that decision.
~ Eleanor Roosevelt

Our Thoughts:

This time in your life is a tough one, where everything is up for examination and everything is in an uproar. Don't forget who you are in the ensuing melee. Stick to your center, hold to it no matter what. This may require some tough self-examination because people coming out of a relationship often don't recall who they are anymore. "I" has become "we" over the years. Take this time to re-examine who you are so you don't inadvertently compromise yourself.

Your Thoughts:

Who am I?

Happiness is not a state to arrive at,
but a manner of traveling.
~ Margaret Lee Runbeck

Our Thoughts:

How about spending more time outdoors? You could stroll around
your neighborhood, or adopt a local park. Walk, listen to the
sounds of the woods, float leaf boats down a creek, and breathe in
the fresh air. Even if you haven't felt drawn to the outdoors, try
immersing yourself in nature. It can be both relaxing and healing –
a gentle pathway to happiness.

Your Thoughts:

Where can I go to tune in to nature?

☯

I'll not listen to reason…Reason always
means what someone else has to say.
~ Elizabeth Gaskell

Our Thoughts:

This is a good time to learn who you are and what's right for you.
You've probably thought right up until the moment divorce
seemed inevitable that *you* were reasonable. Now life is topsy
turvy, and you don't know what to think anymore. There's a part
of you, however, that is your best advisor…your gut feelings.

Your Thoughts:

Do I listen to my gut?

The sorrow which has no vent in tears
may make other organs weep.
~ Henry Maudsley

Our Thoughts:

Allow plenty of time to weep. The tears that *aren't* shed can
cause so much more pain – both physically and emotionally –
than those that are. (Yes, this means you, too, men!)

Your Thoughts:

How difficult is it for me to cry?

❡

Someday we'll look back on this moment and
plow into a parked car.
~ Evan Davis

Our Thoughts:

Ending a relatively comfortable or at least a familiar old life and
beginning a new one takes an astonishing amount of energy, both
physical and emotional. So give yourself a break, and set your
expectations realistically low for the first few weeks. If, in the
course of a day, you (1) consume one "regular" meal, (2) take a
nice nap, and (3) remember to check the mailbox, give yourself a
pat on the back.

Your Thoughts:

How can I expend my energy wisely?

☯

Natural forces within us
are the true healers of disease.
~ Hippocrates

Our Thoughts:

Divorce is not a disease, but it is certainly dis-ease. Nothing about this process is easy, and while it's going on we can experience health problems, emotional upsets and a mind that never shuts up or shuts down. There may be moments when you'll feel that you're drowning in molasses. That's when you need to find those inner resources we all have (yes, all of us) that help you through and guide you in the direction of doing what's necessary to hasten healing.

Your Thoughts:

What can I do today to take care of myself?

☯

The only one who makes no mistakes
is one who never does anything.
~ Theodore Roosevelt

Our Thoughts:

If you are sad and feeling that you're a failure because your
marriage is over, reading this quote over and over again should
help you come to terms with the fact that everyone makes
mistakes. And like it or not, that's how we learn. Take your pain
and benefit from it.

Your Thoughts:

How do I get hung up on being perfect?

☯

One of the greatest necessities in America
is to discover creative solitude.
~ Carl Sandburg

Our Thoughts:

Pity the people who spurn their own company, for they are
destined to be restless. Most creative endeavors – writing, music,
hand work, sculpting, carving, and others – flourish in the quiet
of solitude, even if you have the stereo blasting at break-glass
volume. Here "quiet" refers to the absence of other people's input.
Relaxing into yourself is an effective way to encourage the dance
of your creative muse.

Your Thoughts:

How often and under what circumstances do I enjoy the *absence* of
other people's noises?

Courage is resistance to fear,
mastery of fear –
not absence of fear.
~ Mark Twain

Our Thoughts:

There's a saying: *feel the fear and do it anyway.* We're all afraid of something at various times in our lives, and divorce is undoubtedly one of the most fearful life events there is. Everything is in flux...domicile, finances, child custody, to name but a few. The uncertainty principle is in full force, a situation humans don't handle very well. It's helpful if you can understand that fear is normal and a function of survival. Talk to your fear, make it real for you. Tell it that it's just going to have to come along for the ride!

Your Thoughts:

How do I handle fear?

❦

Someone has said that the greatest cause
of ulcers is mountain-climbing
over molehills.
~ Maxwell Maltz

Our Thoughts:

It's so easy to be dramatic during this time in your life. Sigh.
Choke. Sniff. Many are guilty of overstating the issues, and
exaggeration rules the day. When two people get into those
games, it's horribly chaotic. Back up and get a good grip on
reality (and your sense of humor while you're at it). It's a waste of
energy to take giant leaps over stones in the road.

Your Thoughts:

What issues am I overstating?

❧

Humor is emotional chaos
remembered in tranquility.
~ James Thurber

Our Thoughts:

You'll recall at least parts of this period in your life with humor.
There will even be hilarious things that happen during this time.
You don't see them yet, but you will. And when something funny
does happen...try to laugh! Laughter lightens and lifts the spirit.

Your Thoughts:

Where's the humor in my life today?

❀

What scares me about divorce
is that my children might put me
in a home for unwed mothers.
~ Teressa Skelton

Our Thoughts:

Whether your offspring are small children or adults, they'll need
time to adjust to the break up of their parents. Even if they saw it
coming, even if they are relieved – their world has drastically
changed. Reassure them of your love. Curb the impulse to tell
them what a jerk the other parent is. And give them time.

Your Thoughts:

What "normal" things can the kids and I do together to reassure all
of us that our love hasn't changed?

Never throw mud. You may miss your mark.
And you will certainly have dirty hands.
~ Joseph Parker

Our Thoughts:

Oh, it's so tempting to stab that soon-to-be-ex in the back…telling
tales to the children, friends, co-workers, bosses…air-dropping
a list of his or her sins over your town or city. Resist! Doing this
will only sully your own Self and your reputation as a human
being. You don't want to be a doormat to be trampled …but
defending yourself is different than being malicious. If your
spouse is maligning you, rise above it. It'll be easier to live with
yourself, and others will respect you.

Your Thoughts:

Am I defending myself or being malicious?

☯

The secret of happiness is freedom,
and the secret of freedom,
courage.
~ Thucydides

Our Thoughts:

It may seem you'll never smile again. Finding the courage to go
on in the face of any conflict is a challenge. Even if leaving your
spouse was the best move you ever made, it required courage to do
it. So whether you are the person leaving, or the person left,
freedom to be happy requires uncommon courage.

Your Thoughts:

How courageous am I?

❂

Success is often achieved by those who
don't know that failure is inevitable.
~ Coco Chanel

Our Thoughts:

Whatever success you want in your life is yours for the taking.
Don't dwell on failure. If you make a misstep or even fall in a
hole, just assume it's one of the things you have to do on the way
to succeeding.

Your Thoughts:

How do I get up out of the holes and carry on?

This life is a test; it is only a test.
If it were a real life, you would receive instructions
on where to go and what to do.
~ Unknown

Our Thoughts:

If you feel you're being tested and sorely tried, you're definitely in touch with reality. Divorce is the mother of all tests. It challenges your patience, your sanity, your civility and highlights your coping mechanisms (or the lack thereof). And where *are* those instructions, anyway? Take heart. Like most tests, it has a beginning, a middle and an end. Look for the end.

Your Thoughts:

What instructions can I give myself?

The bird of paradise alights only
upon the hand that does not grasp.
~ John Berry

Our Thoughts:

When our lives change, the first impulse is to grab onto the
familiar and hang on for dear life. Clinging to that which is
changing or disappearing from your life won't keep it near you.
Don't cling to your spouse, your old way of life, your children, or
anything else for that matter. Hold your life in the open palm of
your hand and allow what wants to leave to do so. Whatever
remains is rightfully and truly yours.

Your Thoughts:

Can I let go?

❀

Solitude is un-American.
~ Erica Jong

Our Thoughts:

Coming out of a marriage and communal living can find you alone
in an apartment or house. Even if you have children, the loss of
the companion spouse is deeply felt by most, even if that feeling is
relief. Many divorcing people haven't been alone in years! For
some, the solitude is welcome; for others, it's agonizing. But it's
important to be alone with yourself in order to take stock and
reflect on what needs to be done. Don't be afraid of solitude.
Use it.

Your Thoughts:

What's the best way to utilize my new solitude?

❀

We are always getting ready to live
but never living.
~ Ralph Waldo Emerson

Our Thoughts:

Zen masters encourage students to live fully in the present. If
you're stuck in your past playing "what if" games with yourself, or
churning around in your future playing "ain't it awful," you'll miss
your present life completely. Look around at what's happening
right now, this minute, this second. That's the only time there is.
Don't lose it.

Your Thoughts:

Am I here...now?

❧

Never eat more than you can lift.
~ Miss Piggy

Our Thoughts:

Food is often a comfort in our stress and aloneness. Denying that fact only leads to frustration and is a set-up for perceived failure of self control. Instead learn to be selective. If what your spirit craves is chocolate, don't try to make do with carrot sticks. It won't work. Sometimes we really do need to satisfy that yen to comfort our souls.

Your Thoughts:

What treats – in reasonable amounts – boost my spirits?

☯

When angry, count four;
when very angry, swear.
~ Mark Twain

Our Thoughts:

Better still, find a physical outlet for that anger. One of the hand-
iest venting methods around is stomp walking. Go for a good, long
walk using the same thunderous steps you would if you were
Godzilla crushing Tokyo! Kicking pebbles along the way is good,
too. It's a bit hard on the feet, but an effective rage defuser.

Your Thoughts:

What else besides stomp walking would diffuse the energy of my
anger?

❀

The heroic life is living the
individual adventure.
~ Joseph Campbell

Our Thoughts:

Remember to acknowledge the courage, stamina, and determination within your soul that are moving you forward in the long process of becoming single again. As the days pass and challenges are successfully met you'll feel stronger than you thought possible. And know that, now, you are indeed living an individual adventure.

Your Thoughts:

What challenges have I already faced and overcome in the divorce process?

◐

As soon as you trust yourself,
you will know how to live.
~ Goethe

Our Thoughts:

Feeling a little wobbly lately? Unsteady on your emotional feet?
Now is the time for trust—in yourself and in your innate ability to
withstand the earthquake that is divorce. No matter what your life
situation is at the moment, you're here! You're alive! And you've
gotten yourself to this place. Trust your next steps.

Your Thoughts:

Do I trust myself?

❦

She has lost the art of conversation,
but not, unfortunately, the power of speech.
~ George Bernard Shaw

Our Thoughts:

When your friends ask how you're handling the big transition, odds are they are sincerely interested. But they don't necessarily want a two hour, blow-by-blow update. Practice answering briefly, then move on to what *they* have been up to. This strategy will go a long way to help keep *you* from getting stuck in the travail of divorce and you'll both enjoy a more upbeat conversation.

Your Thoughts:

What one or two sentences can I use to thank friends for their concern?

The time to relax
is when you don't have time for it.
~ Sydney J. Harris

Our Thoughts:

All of us lead busy lives these days. Too busy. Taking time out to relax is always an important stress reliever and it's *especially* important during a divorce. Let something else go—the laundry can wait and so can the dirty dishes. Your life can't wait. Do whatever it is that soothes you.

Your Thoughts:

What are some things that make me feel good?

❧

Why dust the house when you can just wait a
couple of years and get a snow blower?
~ Unknown

Our Thoughts:

Life may be a bit overwhelming right now. Housekeeping falls
into that category. You can obsess and clean all the time (not
healthy) or you can obsess and worry because you're not cleaning
at all (equally unhealthy). Here's a flash: *it doesn't matter!* There
are more important issues at hand. If you can afford it, hire a
housekeeping service. If you can't, clean once a month. If your
friends are visiting your house and not you, they aren't friends.

Your Thoughts:

What is my definition of "clean"?

Protest long enough that you are right,
and you will be wrong.
~ Yiddish proverb

Our Thoughts:

Many divorces are rancorous and ugly. Sometimes both parties
behave like bullies, sometimes only one. When it comes to separating and unraveling, there are plenty of "right" and "wrong"
subjects over which everyone can argue. Focus too long on these
and you'll be at risk for obsessing over minute points that won't
matter in the long run anyway. Know what's possible to accomplish and go for it. Argue over tiny points and you'll find yourself
mired in a long, ugly divorce.

Your Thoughts:

Do I insist on being right?

☯

Change is good…you go first.
~ Judy Highfill, Pamela Picker, Gwen Romire and Mary Stuart
Motto

Our Thoughts:

Change is life. Not to change is to die. Why, then, is it so tough?
Because it's hard work and it upsets our illusory sense of security
that things will go on as they always have. There is no such
guarantee. Our only real security lies in adaptability, and our
ability to flex with change.

Your Thoughts:

How easily do I handle change?

❦

Get your facts first,
and then you can distort them
as much as you please.
~ Mark Twain

Our Thoughts:

Whatever you do, tell your attorney the truth, and tell him or her *all* the facts. Leave nothing out. If you have skeletons in your closet, if your spouse is having an affair, or if *you're* having an affair, you must tell your attorney so she or he won't be sandbagged down the road. *Other* than your attorney, however, button up your lips until the divorce is over. You can let your feelings out as much as you like, but keep the facts to yourself.

Your Thoughts:

What have I neglected to tell my attorney?

☯

Love blinds all men alike,
both the reasonable and the foolish.
~ Menander

Our Thoughts:

Going through a divorce puts you in an extremely vulnerable
place in regard to self-esteem. This is *not* the time to be looking
for your next spouse, because you run the risk of ending up in a
rebound relationship or in one that makes you feel good only for
the moment. It may feel like love, but chances are it's just lust.
Take some "time out" from relationships after your divorce is
through. Take some time for your Self.

Your Thoughts:

How do I feel about getting into another relationship?

❧

Reality is the leading cause of stress
for those in touch with it.
~ Jane Wagner

Our Thoughts:

Welcome to divorceland. This is tough noogies time, folks,
because a divorce is nothing *but* reality. Hard hitting, down and
dirty, roll around in the misery reality. That's the bad news. The
good news is, reality has probably been missing from your life
for a long time, and its reappearance bodes well for your mental
health. And the fact is, after the misery comes some peace and
acceptance, which is the best reality there is.

Your Thoughts:

Am I in touch with the reality of my life?

☯

Come, my friends. 'Tis not too late
to seek a newer world.
~ Alfred, Lord Tennyson

Our Thoughts:

No matter how old you are (or feel), there really is a whole new
world awaiting you. You have only to seek it out and claim it.
Grandma Moses started painting when she was in her eighties.
Most ballet dancers start when they're three or four years
old...Nureyev started when he was 17. They were successful
because they *believed* they could do it and because they *wanted* to
do it, and no matter what others' opinions were they forged ahead.

Your Thoughts:

Do I listen to and believe in myself?

❧

We are what we pretend to be.
~ Kurt Vonnegut, Jr.

Our Thoughts

Personal pride straightens our shoulders, lifts our chins, and helps us to create a make-believe appearance of confidence and strength. It's a bit defiant. It says don't pity me. It says I'm strong. And for now maybe it's lying, but the more you act the part, the closer you'll be to feeling it – and becoming it. Fake it 'til you make it!

Your Thoughts:

What positive mantra or phrase can I repeat to myself when I need to boost my morale?

❧

Lord, give me patience… and hurry!
~ George Robinson Ragsdale

Our Thoughts:

Some people are lucky and have rapid and polite divorces. Others
(probably the majority) have divorces that range from mildly
annoying to an experience that rivals the seventh level of Hell. If
you are anywhere on the continuum of annoying to Hell, you no
doubt have the patience of a gnat. Hang on. Do what you have to
do to ungrit those teeth. Deliverance is at hand.

Your Thoughts:

Am I impatient?

The past must no longer be used as an anvil
for beating out the present and the future.
~ Paul-Emile Borduas

Our Thoughts:

How often do you fashion today's and tomorrow's plans on what
you did a decade ago? Do you order mint chocolate chip ice cream
simply because you always have? Do you check the want ads
under Sales just because you've worked in sales? Now is the time
to try on new ideas. Taste them, roll them around in your mouth,
feel how they would fit into your new life. This is the time for
fresh starts.

Your Thoughts:

In what areas, large and small, can I spread my wings and experiment with change?

All serious daring starts from within.
~ Eudora Welty

Our Thoughts:

Going through a divorce is intimidating. Even if you're very angry and aggressively proactive, the process itself can be stupefying. Thoughts of doing something "daring" may strike terror in your heart. This time of crisis and danger contains the seeds of opportunity. Dare to be the visionary of your own life.

Your Thoughts:

What can I dare in my life?

๏

Simplify!
~ Venus Veritas

Our Thoughts:

Whether you're cleaning out the marital home or moving to a new
space, divorce is a great time to simplify your material life. This
kind of pitching is a great way to vent your anger! Throw out the
moldering magazines and the clothes that won't ever fit you again.
Offer some of the family mementos to your offspring if they're old
enough to enjoy them. Toss out the old tooth brushes, paint cans,
and junk. You'll feel a terrific sense of accomplishment and won't
have to find storage space for all that unnecessary trash.

Your Thoughts:

What am I clinging to that I really could throw out or give away?

❂

Those who cannot remember the past
are condemned to repeat it.
~ George Santayana

Our Thoughts:

It's vital to *process* the disintegration of the marriage so you won't be doomed to repeat those same mistakes. Whether you visit a therapist as a couple for "counseling for closure" or make solo appointments, talk out what went wrong, and how *each* of you contributed to the demise of the union. Rare is the breakup that rests solely on one pair of shoulders. Learn for the future.

Your Thoughts:

How did I contribute to the end of the marriage?

❂

Nothing can bring back the hour,
Of splendor in the grass, of glory in the flower.
~ William Wordsworth

Our Thoughts:

The green leaves and blossoms of yesterday truly are gone. Savor the memory, but now look forward with joy to the opening buds of tomorrow.

Your Thoughts:

In what ways do I see my life opening and blossoming in the next year?

֍

If marriage is the most natural state,
how come married people always look nauseous?
~ Jackie Mason

Our Thoughts:

It never hurts to laugh, especially at yourself and your situation.
People enduring the rigors of divorce often lose their sense of
humor, much to the dismay of those around them. Divorce can be
a terrible ordeal. Lighten the load…laugh out loud.

Your Thoughts:

What can I laugh about today?

❧

Millions long for immortality who do not
know what to do with themselves
on a rainy Sunday afternoon.
~ Susan Ertz

Our Thoughts:

The married state develops a routine and life of its own. Many
find themselves at a loss when they are suddenly on their own
with their routines changed or in some cases gone altogether.
If you are at a loss over what to do with yourself, start thinking
about all those things that you wanted to do when you were a
twosome but didn't have time for. Now is the time.

Your Thoughts:

What did I always want to do, but never had time for?

❧

Start off every day with a smile
and get it over with.
~ W. C. Fields

Our Thoughts:

There will be days when you feel as irascible as W. C. Fields. For some, time out is healing. A retreat into music, books, TV or other at-home relaxation may be just the ticket. For others, spending time with a particularly supportive friend may help take away the crankiness.

Your Thoughts:

What jump-starts my spirits?

Keep the Grump away from your answering machine!
~ Venus Veritas

Our Thoughts:
Our voices are dead giveaways to our emotional state, and you
don't want to sound like Polly (or Paulie) Pathetic on your
answering machine. So keep re-recording your greeting until
there's some sunshine in your voice. The most effective way
to accomplish that is to *smile* while you recite the message. If
that makes you feel silly, all the better – you really will have
laughter in your voice.

Your Thoughts:
What picture or joke can I hold in my mind to lighten my voice?

❧

If you don't learn to laugh at trouble,
you won't have anything to laugh at when you grow old.
~ Ed Howe

Our Thoughts:

Humor is a terrific aid to mental health. Go round up a few friends who have run the divorce gauntlet and swap war stories. The black humor and shared laughter will help you put events into perspective.

Your Thoughts:

Who can I round up to share a pizza and wise cracks about divorce?

PHASE II

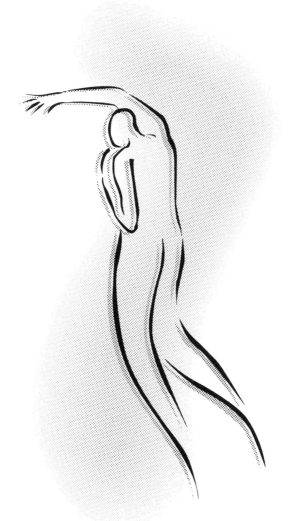

LOOKING OUT

Somebody's boring me...
I think it's me.
~ Dylan Thomas

Our Thoughts:

A long drawn out divorce can produce a litany of woes. You may notice your friends' eyes glazing over or perhaps shifting away from you. Listen to what you are saying to others about your divorce. If you find you're repeating yourself, you're probably boring even you! Find something else to talk about socially. After the first nuclear blast of coming apart and all the concurrent stories, there isn't much to say that isn't repetitious.

Your Thoughts:

Have I become boring?

❂

I find the public passion for justice quite boring and artificial,
for neither life nor nature cares if justice is ever done or not.
~ Patricia Highsmith

Our Thoughts:

Adversaries in divorce actions are quite definite in their views of
justice and fairness. You've heard it before, now hear it again ...
pay attention to what is *actually* happening, not what you think
ought be happening. Getting stuck in what you believe "should"
be occurring will only make you angry and upset because life
rarely happens as we think it "should." It simply happens. If
you can see that clearly, you'll be able to make better decisions.

Your Thoughts:

What is actually occurring now?

☯

> If you don't know where you are going,
> you will probably end up
> somewhere else.
> ~ Laurence J. Peter

Our Thoughts:

How long has it been since you set goals for yourself? Made a life plan? Aimed yourself truly at something you wanted to do, have, or acquire? If you are aimlessly wandering through your life "until the divorce is over," you'll end up in a place that may not be to your liking.

Your Thoughts:

What are my goals?

❂

It wasn't raining
when Noah built the ark.
~ Howard Ruff

Our Thoughts:

Preparation is a great stress reducer! It's having the furnace
checked before cold weather hits, getting your taxes done before
the Ides of April, or catching up with the laundry. An ounce of
preparation will help you avoid a ton of troublesome moments.

Your Thoughts:

What seasonal preparations do I want to mark on my calendar?

☯

Anxiety is the essential condition of
intellectual and artistic creation...
and everything that is finest in human history.
~ Charles Frankel

Our Thoughts:

Enduring a divorce produces great apprehension about a variety
of things from getting out of bed in the morning (can I?) to what
will I do on a date (yikes!). To feel a certain amount of that is
perfectly normal. What is *not* normal is if the anxiety lasts for a
long time and/or immobilizes you. If you fall in the latter category, get professional help before it completely overcomes you.
Otherwise, just know the tension stems from change and the
newness of being single.

Your Thoughts:

Just how anxious am I?

It matters not whether you win or lose;
what matters is whether *I* win or lose.
~ Darrin Weinberg

Our Thoughts:

Beware the quagmire of the divorce settlement! It's common for one or both exiting partners to seek retribution through the division of property. You may feel (and be) justified in claiming more than half in compensation for wrongs done to you in the marriage, but steer clear of pointless revenge for its own sake. Make your decisions based on positive motives and you'll emerge with more self-respect.

Your Thoughts:

What marital assets have I asked for that I don't really want?

❂

The cocktail party – a device for paying off obligations
to people you don't want to invite to dinner.
~ Charles Merrill Smith

Our Thoughts:

When you're ready to rejoin the human race socially, honor your
own comfort level. For some a mixed group of marrieds and
singles, male and female will be the most natural. Others may be
more comfortable with same sex friends – especially those who
have been through the rigors of divorce. Just don't put yourself
into a situation that will be agonizing for you!

Your Thoughts:

Which social gatherings are most comfortable for me right now?

❂

Life is what happens
while you are making other plans.
~ John Lennon

Our Thoughts:

The universe often seems to have a perverse sense of humor.
Control issues immediately rear their ugly little heads during a
divorce, each person trying to maintain a sense of equilibrium by
controlling what happens. It's not that you shouldn't plan for your
future, but you can't wrestle it down and stake it in the ground for
all time. If you try, you'll just be miserable. Let go. Make your
plans, and wait on the will of heaven (or a strange judge).

Your Thoughts:

Am I a controller, or do I let events unfold?

☯

Living is entirely too time-consuming.
~ Irene Peter

Our Thoughts:

The long process of divorce has a way of devouring all the hours
of your week. You're so intent upon the next meeting with the
attorney, or the court date, or that brand new mortgage payment
that before you know it, the year's half gone. Every once in
awhile, reclaim the here and now by gazing at the tree branches
against the blue and clouded sky, or bending to feel the velvet of
the rose petals. Take a few slow, deep breaths along the way, and
you'll feel centered again in real life.

Your Thoughts:

What will be my own version of stopping to smell the roses?

☯

You can't shake hands with a clenched fist.
~ Indira Gandhi

Our Thoughts:

You're angry. Your soon-to-be-ex has just said or done something perfectly unspeakable. Keep your eye on the donut, not the hole…the objective is to get through this divorce the best possible way especially if there are children involved. Keep your anger in check (not stuffed) and retain a cool head. Think with your faculties, not your emotions. Take the latter to your therapist, friends, or minister or whack some cushions with a plastic ball bat. Do *not* spew them in a vitriolic eruption all over everyone. The acid will drive them all away.

Your Thoughts:

How am I managing my anger?

It doesn't matter what you do,
as long as you don't do it in public
and frighten the horses.
~ Mrs. Patrick Campbell

Our Thoughts:

When first in the throes of unraveling a relationship, many discover there's a strong tendency to talk incessantly about what's happening to you. Your really good friends will tolerate this...for a while. Don't impinge on their good will. If you're still weeping, complaining and otherwise beating your breast three months after the initial shock wave, get over it and get on with it. Oh, and thank your friends for their indulgence!

Your Thoughts:

Am I taking advantage of my friends? How?

❧

It's not love that is blind,
but jealousy.
~ Lawrence Durrell

Our Thoughts:

Ah, the green-eyed monster. Never is there more fertile ground for this dragon to rear its ugly little head than a divorce. The possibilities are endless over what you can be jealous of, ranging from feeling that the kids like your spouse better than you, to your spouse's new significant other, or to who got what of the personal effects. Jealousy doesn't change the facts – it only changes your attitude. Determine to let go of the monster.

Your Thoughts:

Am I experiencing jealousy?

❂

I shall let my soul lie fallow,
ignore the hassles,
set aside the multitude of stultifying shoulds,
and
simply
be.
~ Linda C. Senn

Our Thoughts:

In times of major life transitions, we may feel a compelling need to ignore the old and begin the new at Mach 3 with our hair on fire. Such a plan allows no time to simply *be*. Few of us are experienced at living in the moment – we certainly didn't learn it at our parents' knees.

Between the end of the old and the beginning of the new, we need a time out. This is a matter of being with yourself – for days or weeks – in non-competitive, relaxing activities like reading, journaling, walking, biking, and meditating. View it as a mental health break, and make time simply to be.

Your Thoughts:

How can I prepare for an effective time out?

Do not insult the mother alligator
until after you have crossed the river.
~ Haitian proverb

Our Thoughts:

Don't go out of your way to enrage your soon-to-be-ex until the
ink is dry on the decree. Negotiating in anger leaves everybody a
loser.

Your Thoughts:

How can I keep from dumping my anger at my soon-to-be-ex on
my children?

☯

The most courageous act is still
to think for yourself. Aloud.
~ Coco Chanel

Our Thoughts:

This is difficult for many people in our culture, and it requires growing *into* the strength to pull it off. The rewards are vast … you will, in the end, own yourself. Be bold. Be as bad as you wanna be (it probably isn't bad at all, you just think it is). Be creative. Be outrageous. Be your own person.

Your Thoughts:

Do I think for myself? Aloud?

❂

Develop a healthy balance between cerebral
and physical exercise in your new life.
~ Venus Veritas

Our Thoughts:

Move your bones and flex your mind. Balancing your sedentary
pleasures, like reading, with some bone movers like jogging make
for a healthier you. When body and mind are both engaged, the
spirit benefits, too.

Your Thoughts:

How is my life out of balance and how can I remedy that?

❂

Our biological drives are several million
years older than our intelligence.
~ Arthur E. Morgan

Our Thoughts:

The feelings of pain and emptiness that we experience in divorce
make us all hunger for affection. A friend or relative's loving
arms offer safe harbor, but think long and hard before you rush
into a new romance prematurely. There is much healing to be
done before you are ready to enter a new relationship as a whole,
healthy person.

Your Thoughts:

Who can I turn to for hugs and affection without risking a
premature romance?

108

I'm not going to limit myself just because
people won't accept the fact that I can do something else.
~ Dolly Parton

Our Thoughts:

When your lifestyle changes as a result of divorce (and it *does*) you might want to consider reformulating some aspects of your life. You may be met with resistance from everybody in the universe. Nevertheless, follow your heart and your bliss. If you want to do something different, do it! Life is change. Death is status quo.

Your Thoughts:

What do I want to change?

Advice is what we ask for when we already
know the answer but wish we didn't.
~ Erica Jong

Our Thoughts:

If you're hung up in wishful thinking you may not like what you
hear. You might ask a good friend if she or he thinks your personality could stand some improvement, or if a course of action you're
considering might be a really bad idea. If a "yes" response feels
utterly devastating, it's probably because you've suspected it all
along. If your instincts are singing out ... pay attention. They're
probably right. Brace yourself.

Your Thoughts:

Am I asking for advice when I already know the answer?

❧

When one is painting
one does not think.
~ Raphael Sanzio

Our Thoughts:

This statement speaks to losing oneself in a project. During a divorce the mind is in overdrive, thinking thinking thinking, always thinking. Find a project in which to lose yourself in order that you may experience life, feel it, even if only for a few moments. It's important to get out of your head now and again.

Your Thoughts:

What sort of project appeals to me?

❧

Sticks and stones may break my bones,
but names will never hurt me.
~ Childhood Rhyme

Our Thoughts:

Dare to express your own true thoughts, no matter what conventional wisdom tells you, and no matter what names people may slap on you for doing so. Getting through a divorce without being called hateful names is distinctly unlikely. Develop a thicker skin, and know that you will survive.

Your Thoughts:

Do I know how to stand up for myself?

☯

Hasten slowly.
~ Augustus Caesar

Our Thoughts:

As the months of transition pass by, you may become impatient
for all the problems and unfinished business of your life to be
completed once and for all. Now, you say, now I'm ready to
move on! I want all these niggling little worries to be gone. But
time is still the healer, and the problems will sort themselves out
in due course. Engage your senses in a walk outdoors, a quiet time
of music and meditation, or a go-for-broke pickup basketball
game to help modify the impatience.

Your Thoughts:

What are some impatience modifiers that will work for me?

❂

I like the dreams of the future
better than the history of the past.
~ Thomas Jefferson

Our Thoughts:

In trying to deal with pain and grievances that surface in the
process of divorce, it becomes all too easy to live in the past,
resurrecting old wrongs and what ifs. These complex, negative
emotions are best dealt with in the presence of a mental health
professional. Those messages from the past are so confused and
overlaid upon earlier problems, that simply dwelling on them in
solitude does little toward eventual healing. Go over them and set
them aside until a therapist can help you sort out the messages.

Your Thoughts:

What concerns would I share with a good therapist right now?

۞

Let there be spaces in our togetherness.
~ Kahlil Gibran

Our Thoughts:

It's very tempting to jump right out of the frying pan into the fire and find another relationship; resist that temptation. While divorcing you need all your energies focused on what is happening between you and your soon-to-be-ex, as well as on your children and their well being. No matter how old you are there will be time enough for another relationship. Finish one completely before you start another.

Your Thoughts:

Am I focusing my energies on another in order to avoid my present?

You get what you expect.
~ Venus Veritas

Our Thoughts:

It's easy to become negative during a divorce because there is so much about the process that's disturbing and wrenching. Don't get in the habit of expecting everything to be bad. Go hang out with your friends and join in the laughter. Let yourself be swept up in the fun and funny stuff, and allow yourself to forget your drama for a while. Afterward, go home and get a good night's sleep. If you're having trouble sleeping, consult with your health practitioner for either prescription or natural remedies. Don't neglect laughter and sleep.

Your Thoughts:

Have I become negative in my outlook?

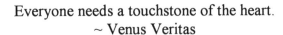

Everyone needs a touchstone of the heart.
~ Venus Veritas

Our Thoughts:

Who in your life – past or present – has been especially encouraging and supportive toward you and your life goals? Your sister? Friend? Grandma? When you need a morale boost, picture that person's smile directed at you. Hear their validating, uplifting words. Better still, dig out a photo, have it framed, and hang it in a place of honor in your new home.

Your Thoughts:

Which people have been the most loving and encouraging to me throughout my life?

☯

The banked fires of day
Gently lead the soul to rest –
> Sunset's amber glow,
Thence the sooty, soft nightfall,
Preceding the pearl of dawn.
~ Linda C. Senn

Our Thoughts:

An after-dark stroll around the neighborhood often puts us in closer touch with nature. Inhale the scent of the summer evening with its perfume of fresh cut grass and the damp smell of sprinklers. Listen to the night creatures, the birds settling in the trees, the crickets, and the rustle of leaves. Look up and see the darkness and the light of the night sky. And relax in nature.

Your Thoughts:

After taking an evening walk, what are my sensory impressions?

❂

Diplomacy is the art of saying "Nice Doggie"
until you can find a rock.
~ Will Rogers

Our Thoughts:

Over the course of the separation and divorce, don't antagonize
your soon-to-be-ex. Marshall your defenses, work with your
attorney and/or mediator, ventilate to your therapist and your
friends, but be neutral in your dealings with the Other. A firm
but pleasant "nice doggie" approach can prevent increased
acrimony, and will go a long way toward smoother negotiations
over property division and custody rights.

Your Thoughts:

How can I vent and diffuse my anger *away* from the Other?

❧

We cherish our friends not for their
ability to amuse us, but for ours to amuse them.
~ Evelyn Waugh

Our Thoughts:

You probably don't feel much like amusing your friends these
days, and that's all right. The reverse of this axiom is true as
well...our friends like to amuse us too. Now is the time to let
them. Of course, humor is a saving grace in any situation and
should you feel the urge to find something funny in your current
life experience, do so! Laughter truly is healing.

Your Thoughts:

What has made me laugh in the last week?

☯

There is no gravity. The earth sucks.
~ Graffito

Our Thoughts:

There's no getting around it. Sometimes *life* sucks, too. Learn a
few effective coping methods to help you deal with anger, like
going for long walks or whacking your mattress with a plastic ball
bat. Stuffing anger just results in emotional constipation, and
that's a major pain.

Your Thoughts:

What are some ways I can cope with my anger?

When the situation is desperate,
it's too late to be serious.
Be playful.
~ Edward Abbey

Our Thoughts:

You've probably spent a great deal of time planning and agonizing
and perhaps even plotting how this divorce and the rest of your life
are going to turn out. If your headache ratio has climbed
alarmingly as a result, take a break. Go swing on a swing, walk on
the beach, eat breakfast at dinnertime. Whatever floats your boat.
If you don't know how to play, go watch some kids or better yet,
play with them. They'll teach you.

Your Thoughts:

Do I know how to play?

❀

As a drop of oil on the sea,
you must float,
using intellect and compassion
to ride the waves.
~ Joseph Campbell

Our Thoughts:

Bringing your seasoned intelligence into play will eventually
produce logical solutions to the practical problems of becoming
single again. But in the process of coping, remember to extend
the same loving compassion to yourself that you do to your
dearest friends.

Your Thoughts:

How can I be kinder to myself?

There is glory in a great mistake.
~ Nathalia Crane

Our Thoughts:

People often view their ending marriages as having been "mistakes." Perhaps they were. Often, however, these relationships simply reflect where a person was in his or her growth at the time. The glory in mistakes is contained in the lessons we learn and the growth we experience.

Your Thoughts:

By what means can I measure my growth?

❂

Good breeding consists in concealing
how much we think of ourselves
and how little we think of the other person.
~ Mark Twain

Our Thoughts:

It's very tempting, particularly in a nasty divorce scenario, to lay waste to your spouse in any way you can…with your children, your joint friends, and (if you're famous) to the general public. Try to resist this impulse, especially around your children. The only person who will be hurt will be you.

Your Thoughts:

What are my nasty thoughts?

☯

Everything is in a state of flux,
including the status quo.
~ Robert Byrne

Our Thoughts:

The status quo is an illusion – a fine example of wishful thinking.
Since change is inevitable, we might just as well embrace it as an
opportunity for growth.   Your divorce may have meant moving to
a new home at a time when you least wanted to be uprooted from
familiar surroundings. But wait! You might discover a great Thai
restaurant near your new digs, or a community theater where you
can volunteer to help behind the scenes or in front of the audience,
or a friend you haven't met yet. Anguishing over change is a
waste of emotional energy – how much better to grow and enjoy!

Your Thoughts:

What new places and opportunities could I explore?

☯

We're all in this alone.
~ Lily Tomlin

Our Thoughts:

There'll come a time when you want a change of scenery, and all your friends are otherwise occupied. So what's a wild, single person to do? Invite *yourself* out to a movie or dinner, that's what! Rush Hour Special movies and Early Bird Special dinners are about half the price of prime time outings, and are just as much fun. Take a book, a notebook, or a small sketchpad and enjoy the company of a fascinating single person – you!

Your Thoughts:

Where will I test my solo wings?

☯

There is always inequity in life.
Some men are killed in a war and some men are wounded,
and some men never leave the country....
Life is unfair.
~ John F. Kennedy

Our Thoughts:

Somehow our culture has encouraged us to believe that life *should*
be fair, and therefore we come to expect that life *will* be fair. Well,
it's official—life isn't fair, and if you're counting on that in your
life and specifically in your divorce, you'll be very disappointed.
Make the very best plans you can, take care of yourself, and await
events.

Your Thoughts:

How can I take care of myself?

❧

Peace is not only better than war,
but infinitely more arduous.
~ George Bernard Shaw

Our Thoughts:

Let's face it – you're testy these days. For a while people will make allowances, but eventually that chip on your shoulder is going to produce major splinters, both in the work place and in social settings. So you had better learn to swallow those nasty remarks. Either come up with alternative, neutral comments or just be quiet. However difficult it may be to throttle back the anger, it's easier than constant fence mending. Take your anger to the basketball court or to a good therapist.

Your Thoughts:

Where and how can I safely turn my anger loose?

ꙮ

The intellect is always fooled
by the heart.
~ La Rochefoucauld

Our Thoughts:

There is a saying in the various 12-step programs that "Intelligence" over "Emotion" is always the preferred state. Not that you shouldn't follow your heart, but in times of stress, you need to be able to think clearly and lucidly, or your "E" may lead you astray. If you find yourself awash in a flood of feelings, beware ... you may make bad decisions during those times. Take a moment for yourself. Take a deep breath. Count to 10. Count as high as you need to count. When you think you have a grip, carry on.

Your Thoughts:

How am I "I" over "E" or "E" over "I"?

๏

The wish for healing has ever been half of health.
~ Seneca

Our Thoughts:

Want it badly enough, and you'll get it. Daily affirmations for health, both mental and physical, will help make this trying time less difficult and definitely healthier. Picture yourself in your mind's eye as the most perfect being possible – mentally, physically and spiritually. Picture it in the present. Bring it into being *now.*

Your Thoughts:

What positive affirmations can I create?

☯

A good problem statement often includes:
(a) what is known, (b) what is unknown,
and (c) what is sought.
~ Edward Hodnett

Our Thoughts:

A logical approach can tame even the most stubborn problem.
Whether you use the above problem statement or the old-fashioned
Franklin list (showing the pro's on one side of the paper and the
con's on the other), writing down the facts in some rational order
can reduce most problems to a manageable size.

Your Thoughts:

On which of my current dilemmas could I use the Franklin list?

Happiness is good health and
a bad memory.
~ Ingrid Bergman

Our Thoughts:

It's often been said that if women could recall childbirth clearly there would be only one child to a family! We've all experienced the fading of bad memories and the brilliant recollection of good ones. As bad as your divorce experience may be, in time it will fade. If this *doesn't* happen, you're clinging to unhealthy feelings and may need to find an outlet for expression … seek counsel of those wiser than yourself.

Your Thoughts:

What bad feelings can I let go of today?

Survival is the ability to swim
in strange water.
~ Frank Herbert

Our Thoughts:

When you've been married for a time, whatever time that may
be, a comfort zone develops around the married life. Even in bad
unions, there is a certain comfort in the familiarity of just how
bad it is. When the divorce process begins, you are indeed in
uncharted territory. Even if you've been divorced before, this
current one is its own creature. Instead of being terrified of the
water, think about all the things you might discover in the
process of swimming in *new* water.

Your Thoughts:

How will I know when I'm ready to take the plunge?

❧

Brain-fried. Open wide…
there's bound to be a thought inside,
deep inside that cranial hole.
Where's my mind,
I'd like to know?
~ Linda C. Senn

Our Thoughts:

During separation and divorce you may find that you're a whole
lot stupider than usual. In other words, temporarily brain-fried. At
some point during the legal maneuverings you'll benefit greatly
from a time out – an interval. Leave home for a few days, even if
it's simply to stay at an in-town, across the way motel. You'll be
away from the phone, the doorbell, and all your "shoulds."

Your Thoughts:

Where can I go for a few days for a mental health break?

He has the gift of quiet.
~ John Le Carre

Our Thoughts:

When you feel completely inundated with plans, appointments and continual input from helpful friends, a simple way to find peace and clear your emotional vision is to meditate. Sit comfortably, close your eyes, and take a few slow, deep breaths. Then picture a comfort place from your past – a wooded glen, a sandy beach, or the corner of your grandmother's couch. Relax in the memory, and when you open your eyes, your vision may again be clear.

Your Thoughts:

What shall I envision as my comfort place?

๏

He who laughs, lasts.
~ Mary Pettibone Poole

Our Thoughts:

Lighten up! Laughter is life. It's too easy to get mired in the
drama of it all and forget there is a funny, lighter side. Yes,
even during divorce! If you've become droopy and dreary, go
see a comedy at the local movie house, or rent one. Go to a
comedy club. Read jokes. Hang out with people who are happy
and laugh a lot. If you can't manage any of this, you're probably
depressed … seek help.

Your Thoughts:

What is the funny side of this divorce?

❦

An IRS audit is a piece of cake compared to
reentering the strange new world of dating.
~ Venus Veritas

Our Thoughts:

If you were married for less than five years, the rules of dating may
not have changed too radically. But if you've been out of the loop
for a decade or two, be aware that the old rules no longer apply.
"Interview" other once-again-single people to get a feel for the
vagaries of dating in your area. (New York guidelines might not
be particularly effective in Topeka.) And then relax. Consider both
your date's comfort level and your own, and if you're still unsure,
fess up. He or she may feel as awkward as you do.

Your Thoughts:

What dating questions do I want to put to my single-again friends?

❧

To thine own self be true.
~ William Shakespeare

Our Thoughts:

It's easy to lose your focus during a divorce. There are all kinds
of feelings and events that can draw your attention away: anger,
fear, details of life in general. It's easy to forget the primary
issue of "where am I in all of this?" When in doubt about any
issue at hand, listen to that still, small voice deep within you. It
always knows best and will guide you faithfully.

Your Thoughts:

What is my inner voice telling me?

☯

My husband and I didn't sign a prenuptial agreement.
We signed a mutual suicide pact.
~ Roseanne Barr Arnold

Our Thoughts:

Roseanne knows whereof she speaks. Divorcing a spouse, or
being divorced by one, can be compared to a free fall off a cliff
sans parachute. People have likened divorce to being murdered,
killed, dismembered and other unpleasant atrocities. Sometimes
the two people involved are primarily interested in inflicting pain
in the process of exiting. If you value your sanity and your
integrity (you have to look in the mirror every day, after all) take
the high road even if you're being savaged. This doesn't mean
you should be a whipping post …defend your rights, but don't
maul your spouse no matter how tempting it may be.

Your Thoughts:

Am I taking the high road?

❂

A good laugh and a long sleep
are the best cures
in the doctor's book.
~ Irish Proverb

Our Thoughts:

"A priest, a rabbi and a minister"... you hear these words, you
know a joke is coming. Laughter comes from many sources, and
should be enjoyed even in the worst of times (all those feel-good
endorphins flow from laughter as well as tears). Don't hang onto
your pain and angst just because you think you should. That only
makes you a martyr, and as we all know the only good martyrs are
dead. So laugh your head off – deep, gut twisting belly laughs, if
possible. Laugh until you cry (more endorphins). And then be
sure to get a good night's sleep, preferably with a smile on your
lips.

Your Thoughts:

When have I laughed lately?

❂

It is a mistake to look too far ahead. Only one link
in the chain of destiny can be handled at a time.
~ Winston Churchill

Our Thoughts:

During the period of separation, we're focused primarily on getting past the old and into the new. Emotionally bound up in the
bewildering fog of legalities, we have neither the time nor the
energy for goals beyond the Day of the Decree. Don't fret – it's
OK. When the clouds begin to lift, you will see the vast possibilities of your future. That will be the time to explore new goals.

Your Thoughts:

Which of my goals can I set aside until the fog lifts?

❂

During your marriage, did socializing always mean
a pot luck dinner at another couple's house?
~ Venus Veritas

Our Thoughts:

When you first emerge into the grand and scary world of single-
dom, you may feel the social rug has been jerked out from under
you. No more are you part of a couple. The good news is there's
a wealth of activities and events out there that don't require a
Noah's ark approach. Check your newspaper for art gallery
openings, fairs, lectures, dance lessons, and a host of diverse
offerings. Try to attend something new at least once a month.

Your Thoughts:

What events do I want to check out?

In the face of an obstacle which is
impossible to overcome,
stubbornness is stupid.
~ Simone de Beauvoir

Our Thoughts:

Pick your battles. Pick them carefully. If you're engaged in a
dogfight where your defeat is certain, you're just wasting precious
energy. Since we all know life isn't fair, sticking with a battle plan
just because you're in the right and it *should* go your way will just
get you soundly whipped. There are times when you must give
way. There are times when you must *not* give way. Wisdom lies
in knowing the difference.

Your Thoughts:

Do I know the difference?

☯

If Patrick Henry thought that taxation without representation was bad, he should see how bad it is with representation.
~ The Old Farmer's Almanac

Our Thoughts:

Speaking of which, the IRS will still expect your cooperation regardless of how shredded you feel inside and out. If you're uncertain about preparing your income taxes that first April of flying solo, seek the services of an accountant or CPA at least for that year. There are enough stresses going on in your life right now without dodging the Feds.

Your Thoughts:

What can I do now to make tax time less stressful?

Change your thoughts and you change your world.
~ Norman Vincent Peale

Our Thoughts:

It's so easy to get stuck in a stale, outdated mindset. As long as you're beginning a new life, be genuinely open to fresh ideas and philosophies. The theory you bad-mouthed last year may turn out to be a fascinating topic for exploration now. The more open you are to new ideas, the greater life's possibilities will seem. After all, your outlook on life is an essential element of who you are.

Your Thoughts:

What people in my life can introduce me to fresh, unfamiliar interests?

❧

Moral courage is a more rare commodity than
bravery in battle or great intelligence.
~ Robert F. Kennedy

Our Thoughts:

In establishing your new self you may need greater than normal
courage to redefine who you are. Those who are close to you may
have trouble with the changes, but it's essential to your personal
growth and integrity to honor the real you. As kindly as possible
tell them to deal with it!

Your Thoughts:

What positive changes in my life will take the greatest moral
courage on my part?

Male sexual response is far brisker and more automatic;
It is triggered easily by things, like
putting a quarter into a vending machine.
~ Alex Comfort

Our Thoughts:

This isn't sexist … it's a biological truth. And it's well for all concerned to bear in mind. Men, don't be led into an emotionally dangerous situation just because your enthusiasm is up. And women, don't mistake a purely sexual invitation for deep and abiding love.

Your Thoughts:

How can I protect my head and heart when I'm in a sexual situation?

❂

Sleep that knits up the ravell'd sleave of care.
~ William Shakespeare

Our Thoughts:

In today's hectic world, sleep seems to be considered optional by some. But medical science has reaffirmed that we need about eight hours sleep per night, that naps are good, and that you can, indeed, make up for lost sleep. A great deal of physical and psychological maintenance and repair goes on while we're in the land of nod, so don't shortchange yourself on zzzz's.

Your Thoughts:

How can I fit more healing sleep time into my life?

❷

Money-giving is a very good criterion...
of a person's mental health.
Generous people are rarely mentally ill people.
~ Karl A. Menninger

Our Thoughts:

Generosity goes way beyond merely handing out money, which some of us don't have. That doesn't mean we don't have something to give. Generosity of *spirit* is important while enduring the pain of divorce, so try viewing your soon-to-be-ex in a spirit of generosity and see what happens.

Your Thoughts:

How am I generous of spirit?

☯

The way I see it, if you want the rainbow,
you gotta put up with the rain.
~ Dolly Parton

Our Thoughts:

There is always something good about adversity, whether or not
you can see it at the time. A door closes ... here; one opens ...
there. If you are drowning in rain, look up ... you might see the
rainbow.

Your thoughts:

What doors are closing? What doors are opening?

Life is so unlike theory.
~ Anthony Trollope

Our Thoughts:

Life just loves to detour around our solutions and scenarios –
premature bridge crossing is often a waste of mental and emotional
energy, especially if you're trying to second-guess the facts.
Living through and surviving a divorce makes clear the difference
between what is and what's theory.

Your Thoughts:

What bridges am I crossing prematurely?

❦

Some people are like popular songs
that you only sing for a short time.
~ La Rochefoucauld

Our Thoughts:

As you begin life as a single, you'll meet a great many new people.
Learn from them, enjoy them, but don't expect that each person
will become a bosom buddy. Sometimes others are meant to touch
our lives only briefly and then move on.

Your Thoughts:

Whom have I known briefly, yet learned a great deal from?

The nose knows.
~ Venus Veritas

Our Thoughts:

If your cologne or after shave stirs up painful memories every
time you uncork the bottle, pitch what you have and shop for a
new fragrance. It's time to start some new memories. Make it
a small adventure, spritzing your wrists with tester bottles when
you walk through the local department and drug stores until you
find one that pleases you.

Your Thoughts:

Where shall I go for my cologne/after shave testing?

❂

Ultimately, love is self-approval.
~ Sondra Ray

Our Thoughts:
In order to love yourself, you have to like who you are. Make no mistake … it's important to love your Self, for without it you can't love anyone else.

Your Thoughts:
Do I like and approve of myself?

Let us never negotiate out of fear,
but let us never fear to negotiate.
~ John F. Kennedy

Our Thoughts:

Negotiation and compromise aren't really comfortable areas for
one who is wobbling on the foal's legs of new personhood. We
feel we must *assert* in order to define ourselves, both to others
and ourselves. Mutual give-and-take helps us stretch our flexibility without going through the old process of subverting our
position. The development of that life skill helps guide us to
healthy communication. Assertiveness and compromise are not
mutually exclusive!

Your Thoughts:

How can I stand *up* for myself without standing *on* somebody
else's throat?

❂

A bore is a man who,
when you ask him how he is,
tells you.
~ Bert Leston Taylor

Our Thoughts:

Your friends will listen to your tales of woe…for a while. They will sympathize with you…for a while. They will cluck over you and otherwise offer their shoulders for your tears…for a while. Be aware of when you begin to repeat yourself and whine. If your friends start to avoid you or change the subject abruptly when you once again tune up for your story, take the hint and shut up.

Your Thoughts:

Objectively, how does my story sound to me?

☯

What you want now
is a kneady professional!
~ Venus Veritas

Our Thoughts:

Professional massage offers a healthy, relaxing fix for our natural
need for human touch. If this appeals to you, look for a massage-
therapist-in-training – they charge less than one with extensive
experience and feel just as good. Ask friends and colleagues for
a recommendation.

Your Thoughts:

What do I knead?

❧

The more independent you want to be,
the more generous you must be with yourself
as a woman [man].
~ Diane von Furstenburg

Our Thoughts:

Both genders have difficulty with this concept, especially during
the tension of a divorce. Now is the time to be generous with
yourself...even if it's only to grab time for a nap or a walk in the
park. Be especially kind to yourself emotionally. Generosity of
spirit extends to our *own* souls. You've made mistakes ... so
what? You're human. You might also want to think how this
applies to your soon-to-be-ex.

Your Thoughts:

Am I able to either become independent or regain my
independence?

◉

All are but parts of one stupendous whole,
whose body Nature is, and God the soul.
~ Alexander Pope

Our Thoughts:

The natural progress of the seasons can guide us in accepting the ebbs and flows of transition. Much as you'd like to bundle up your problems and cram them through a solution machine, life doesn't happen that way. As the followers of the Tao have long known, following the rhythm of the seasons can have a calming and steadying effect on the psyche. Try to find time to savor nature's changes – the foraging of the worm-hungry robins, the heavy glare of the sun, those simple changes we encounter every day. The relative constancy of nature is reassuring in times of personal upheaval.

Your Thoughts:

What seasonal changes have I noticed this week?

One ringie dingie....
~ Lily Tomlin

Our Thoughts:

It's unwise to sit around waiting for friends to telephone. They may feel awkward, no matter how much they care. Pick up the phone and *call* someone when you feel ready to venture out of your cave. Chances are they'll be glad you made the overture.

Your Thoughts:

Who would I like to reconnect with in the next month?

❃

Not only is life a bitch, it has puppies.
~ Adrienne A. Gusoff

Our Thoughts:

Okay. You're feeling sorry for yourself. You've worked up a
fever pitch of depression. You've worked hard to get there and
you *by God* intend to enjoy rolling around in the misery. Go
ahead. Indulge. *For a while.* Solo or with only a very good
friend. But don't drag out the drama, or you'll lose your friends
and your mind, and your mood will sink to an all-time low.

Your Thoughts:

Am I in the throes of a pity party?

❦

In this business you either sink or swim
or you don't.
~ David Smith

Our Thoughts:

Invest your energies in the *process* of growing and making a
fresh start. Don't get hung up on outcomes. The former allows
you to take one day and project at a time, living in each forward
movement. The latter implies success or failure. If you've grown
in the process, there is no such thing as failure.

Your Thoughts:

What processes do I already take joy in regardless of the outcome?

❂

I envy people who drink. At least they have
something to blame everything on.
~ Oscar Levant

Our Thoughts:

There's nothing wrong with social drinking. However, if you're
drinking more than usual to relieve stress and emotional pain or
to help you sleep, you might want to step back and assess just
how you might be using alcohol as a crutch. If alcohol has been
an issue for you previously, take care…now is an especially
vulnerable time and relapses happen in the blink of an eye.

Your Thoughts:

What are my emotional crutches?

❀

I don't say that we ought to all misbehave,
but we ought to look as if we could.
~ Orson Welles

Our Thoughts:

Get in touch with your mischievous side, and do something that
would ordinarily be outrageous for you. No, don't do anything
that might jeopardize your position in the divorce action; do
something fun and outside the scope of your normal behavior.
Stretch yourself beyond your limits. Some of us haven't done
this for decades. It's time.

Your Thoughts:

What am I afraid to try?

There are no strangers here –
only friends we have not met.
~ Laurence J. Peter

Our Thoughts:

As you move into your new life, you will meet new people – it's inevitable if you open your life to new possibilities. Think of all the new friends just waiting for you to discover them! Get out into the world and find them...join a church, club, social organization, volunteer your time to a worthy cause...whatever floats your boat. But don't be afraid to move among strangers.

Your Thoughts:

Is there anything stopping me from making new friends?

❧

My marriage didn't work out. I was a human being
and he was a Klingon.
~ Carol Liefer

Our Thoughts:

No matter which gender you are, it's tempting to frame your
spouse as an alien. He or she is the one doing all those weird
things, not you! You've spent a lot of time with this person.
Now that they're officially on the other side of intimacy doesn't
mean they're non-human! Reverse the sentence...and *you*
become the Klingon.

Your Thoughts:

How does that reversal feel?

◉

> I am a deeply superficial person.
> ~ Andy Warhol

Our Thoughts:

Reentering the dating scene is certainly an experience. Some enjoy singles' mixers and dances, while for others those feel like meat markets where bodies meet but minds and spirits are noticeably absent. You'll encounter a great deal of superficial socializing, especially at happy hours. Which is not to say you should avoid such functions – just be aware of the level of interaction that goes on there.

Your Thoughts:

What are some good and bad conversation starters?

Let us run with patience the race
that is set before us.
~ Hebrews 12:1

Our Thoughts:

Slogging through a divorce can seem like an interminable process.
You may feel you'll never see the light of day again. You may be
awash, even drowning in bad feelings and worse thoughts. Days
may go by, then months and still it drags on. Know that progress
is often measured in seconds, and that you can get through the next
second, the next minute, hour, and day. Congratulate yourself for
making it through to the next step.

Your Thoughts:

What congratulatory statements can I make?

Divorce is a game played by lawyers.
~ Cary Grant

Our Thoughts:

Lawyers can sometimes forget who they're working for. If yours makes that error, put a choke chain on her or him, and give it a good yank once in awhile. That'll remind them to keep you up to date on their progress on the case.

Your Thoughts:

Does my attorney keep me informed?

☯

Nothing great was ever achieved
without enthusiasm.
~ Ralph Waldo Emerson

Our Thoughts:

Attitude can make all the difference in the quality of your days.
Let your natural curiosity lead you into new, unexplored areas
of interest. Nurture the happy spark of discovery and learning,
and your outlook will be far more upbeat than if you wallow in
negative thoughts.

Your Thoughts:

What unexplored idea or interest makes my face light up and my
curiosity swell?

❂

> It's a naïve wine without any breeding,
> but I think you'll be amused by its presumption.
> ~ James Thurber

Our Thoughts:

Looking for new, inexpensive places to mingle as a single? Try attending some wine tastings. Call the local wine shops, quality restaurants, and wineries to see when they have tastings scheduled. Community colleges often run wine classes in cooperation with local merchants. You'll find a mix of marrieds and singles – and the conversation topic is built in. It's a good activity for getting your social feet wet.

Your Thoughts:

Which wine shops and adult evening courses in my area offer wine tasting classes?

❂

> There is nothing
> more powerful than habit.
> ~ Ovid

Our Thoughts:

During your married life, you inevitably acquired "married habits," some of which may have been good but don't serve you very well in your single state. Review what you habitually do and how you do it. Ask yourself which behaviors you want to eliminate. One of the most insidious of all is lapsing back into "that old married behavior" when you're around your soon-to-be-ex. Caretaking, fighting postures, last gasp passion and even shared laughter can ambush you if you aren't on your toes.

Your Thoughts:

What are my "married habits"?

PHASE III

LOOKING UP

❦

> You can't make a baby in a month
> by getting nine women pregnant.
> ~ Anonymous

Our Thoughts:

There are some processes you just cannot rush. Producing offspring is one; recovering from divorce is another. Take time to heal, and to give birth to the new, single person that you are now becoming.

Your Thoughts:

In what ways am I trying to rush through this divorce passage?

❦

I have often depended on the blindness of strangers.
~ Adrienne E. Gusoff

Our Thoughts:

If it weren't for friends turning a blind eye (and a deaf ear) to all those tales of woe, there wouldn't be anyone to listen to your Divorce Drama. Remember those friends when you are able to think straight again. Thank them profusely for their patience, and pass the favor on whenever any of your friends go through the same experience. Remember where you came from.

Your Thoughts:

Which friends are being extraordinarily kind to me?

❧

There is nourishment and belonging
in the human touch.
~ Venus Veritas

Our Thoughts:

You say you're hungry for human touch, but aren't ready for a
relationship? Well, you could join a dance group or take a class.
Watch for dancing groups and/or lessons that don't require you
to bring a partner. This congenial activity doesn't have that nasty
"meat market" feeling, and it's great exercise!

Your Thoughts:

What kinds of dancing would I like to try?

❧

It is not true that life is one damn thing after another...
it's the same damn thing over and over again.
~ Edna St. Vincent Millay

Our Thoughts:

Mental health practitioners often cite this definition as the difference between sanity and insanity: sanity is one thing after another, insanity is the same thing over and over again. Take a hard look at your life and see if you're repeating the same damned mistakes over and over. If you have difficulty sorting them out, seek professional assistance. Life should be one damn thing *after* another!

Your Thoughts:

Do I repeat myself, repeat myself, repeat myself?

☯

A wise man will make more
opportunities than he finds.
~ Francis Bacon

Our Thoughts:

Although all the changes that take place at the beginning of a
newly single life can be powerfully daunting, you can't wait for
the world to tap on your door. Actively placing yourself in new
situations with new people can advance your personal growth
process.

Your Thoughts:

Where can I go to meet new people?

☯

It may take some planning to feel
at home in your new solo life.
~ Venus Veritas

Our Thoughts:

It takes some effort to become comfortable with your own
company, but small, new at-home diversions can be fun. Have
you tried crosswords or other puzzles lately? How about reading,
wood carving, TV travel shows, sketching, surfing the web, or
needlework? Find activities you really look forward to coming
home to.

Your Thoughts:

What hobbies and activities would I like to try in my new life?

On my
Walk this evening
I heard the cicadas
High in the huge old shingle oak,
Calling.

Their chants
Promise autumn,
Foretell the coming of
Crispy leaves and crunchy apples
And school.
~ Linda C. Senn

Our Thoughts:

When restlessness overwhelms you, try one of the following:

Call a friend or an emotionally safe relative and ask how *he or she* is.

Drop a note to an out of town pal.

Put a CD on and dance naked in front of the fireplace.

Your Thoughts:

How will I deal with my next episode of restlessness?

☯

Laughter is a tonic
for the weary soul.
~ Venus Veritas

Our Thoughts:

Well, yes – laughter *can* lighten the spirit. It's not that we doubt it
– it's just that humor can be elusive when the soul journeys in pain.
You become more attuned to the witty and whimsical if you begin
keeping a humor journal. Try tucking a small notepad in your
pocket and jot down those things that bring a smile to your face in
the course of the day. Even if you only manage to record a few,
rereading them will return the smile, and you'll wind up paying
more attention to humor if you're watching for it.

Your Thoughts:

What kind of humor most appeals to me?

Dreaming permits each and every one of us
to be quietly and safely insane
every night of our lives.
~ William C. Dement

Our Thoughts:

A dream journal can be fun! It's best to record your dreams as soon as you awaken, for if you wait until later you'll have forgotten what you meant to remember. If you have a therapist, take your journal to some of the sessions for interpretation. You can learn a great deal about yourself.

Your Thoughts:

What are the last few dreams I remember?

❧

I don't know the key to success,
but the key to failure is trying to please everybody.
~ Bill Cosby

Our Thoughts:

In the process of establishing a new place in the world, there
may be a natural tendency to seek the approval of others. After
all, approval is a form of affection, isn't it? But the real secret
is to identify those aspects of yourself that *you* want to develop.
Be true to yourself, and those who are worthy will cheer you on.

Your Thoughts:

How can I begin to value my *own* approval over that of others?

☯

Why beholdest thou the mote that is in
thy brother's eye, but considerest not
the beam that is in thy own eye?
~ Matthew 7:2-3

Our Thoughts:

It's so easy to place blame for a marriage dissolving. How hard
could it be? Isn't it the "other's" fault? Those flaws and issues
are easy to spot, and even easier to focus on, because it lets you
off the hook from examining your part in it. Maybe your spouse
is perfectly awful. That still doesn't let you off the hook. Take
some time to look at yourself, closely. Then see if you can't find
at least one good thing to say about your soon-to-be-ex.

Your Thoughts:

Can I say anything good about my soon-to-be-ex?

☯

But what will we talk about?
~ Venus Veritas

Our Thoughts:

One of the scariest parts of dating again is simply *meeting* new people. And once you and that Fascinating Stranger have made eye contact, how can you move things forward? One way is to look for a conversation piece like an item of jewelry they're wearing or the newspaper they're carrying. Better still, wear a conversation piece yourself which will make it far easier for that stranger to step forward and get acquainted with you.

Our Thoughts:

What clothing, jewelry, book or other items of interest would be good conversation starters for me to use?

❧

Consistency requires you to be as ignorant today
as you were a year ago.
~ Bernard Berenson

Our Thoughts:

Some say that mindless consistency is the same as being in a rut.
That's not a bad thing, but you don't want to spend your whole
life there – even if it's a good rut! A divorce decree legalizes a
fresh start for both parties. Make a list of things you've wanted
to do, but haven't had the time for. As the opportunities arise,
sign up, go out, join in new challenges and activities. Some will
be fun, some will be disappointing. Who cares? You'll feel
adventurous and in control of your own life.

Your Thoughts:

What shall I include in my want-to-do list?

❧

You can always tell a real friend: when you've
made a fool of yourself he doesn't
feel you've done a permanent job.
~ Laurence J. Peter

Our Thoughts:

Friends are your greatest assets. It's been noted by others who
have gone before that during a divorce you find out who your true
friends really are. And it's a good thing, too. Who would want to
go through life thinking someone was on their side who wasn't?
So when the shared friends shuffle around, be thankful for the
ones who stick by you. They're true blue.

Your Thoughts:

Who are my real friends?

The hole and the patch should be commensurate.
~ Thomas Jefferson

Our Thoughts:

Let the solution fit the problem. You don't call out the National Guard to squelch a gopher uprising, no matter how annoyed you are. Likewise, many of the challenges we face in the process of starting over respond best to simple solutions. You can feel just as much in control by letting time, rationality, and nature do the job as you would by rushing around in search of a *big* solution.

Your Thoughts:

Which of my nagging problems would lend themselves to simple solutions?

❧

Listen to a man of experience;
thou wilt learn more in the woods than in books.
~ St. Bernard

Our Thoughts:

Because nature engages all our senses if we let it, a walk in the woods allows us to shed the noisome, peripheral garbage that muddies our thoughts. You can learn a great deal about nature *and* you might learn even more about yourself.

Your Thoughts:

What are my favorite sounds of nature?

❂

> Develop your intuition,
> Hear your gut feelings,
> Honor their guidance,
> And give thanks for the wisdom.
> ~ Linda C. Senn

Our Thoughts:

In recent years society has tended to undervalue that which cannot be analyzed, touched, or reduced to a formula. Intuition, however, has been a reliable guiding force since the dawn of humanity. Comprised of an unconscious store of experience, learning, observation, and perhaps collective memory it deserves your full attention. Hunches are our friends.

Your Thoughts:

What gut feelings have I paid attention to lately, either at work or socially?

❂

When they said "Make love, not war" at Woodstock,
they never imagined that one
would become as dangerous as the other.
~ Jay Leno

Our Thoughts:

If you've been married for a long time, emerging into today's
dating scene is a shock. You may not feel like dating right now, or
you may already be into the thick of it. Eventually, most divorced
people venture out into that world again. The caveat: have fun,
and be careful.

Your Thoughts:

How do I feel about dating again?

❂

Isn't it nice the way kindness begets kindness?
~ Venus Veritas

Our Thoughts:

Friends and family will astonish you with their kindness, patience, and support. And through the first phase of your separation, you'll do well just to accept their gentle ministrations. In time, though, you'll want to express your thanks. Two easy ways to do that are (1) to pass along that kindness to the next friend in need of support, and/or (2) treat the help givers. You can do the latter by taking them out for brunch or dinner or by inviting them to your place for dessert or a pizza party. Keep it simple, and you'll discover the enjoyment of being on the giving end again.

Your Thoughts:

How can I thank those who have stood by me?

❦

Art is the difference between seeing
and just identifying.
~ Jean Mary Norman

Our Thoughts:

As art imitates life, so a quality life can be the difference between seeing, really seeing, and just identifying an object. During a divorce, seeing events and people as they really are rather than just labeling them as "bad" or "good" helps the process considerably.

Your Thoughts:

How clearly am I "seeing"?

Hiking can be great social exercise.
~ Venus Veritas

Our Thoughts:

Some folks prefer the solitude of a private stroll, and some seek to join others along the foot paths and bike trails. You can check the YMCA and your newspaper calendar sections for announcements about walking clubs. Youth Hotels International (formerly American Youth Hostels) offers both bicycling and walking group activities. Give your local office a call.

Your Thoughts:

Which groups and organizations in my area can I contact?

❂

The divorce will be gayer than the wedding.
~ Colette

Our Thoughts:

For most people this is strictly tongue in cheek, Colette notwithstanding. There are, of course, exceptions. For men and women who have been in abusive relationships, this is absolutely true. If you are among this number, take heart…your life will improve substantially when you start over on your own, no matter how difficult the obstacles. If you're the abuser, get help.

Your Thoughts:

What am I feeling about this divorce?

❃

I learned courage from Buddha, Jesus, Lincoln, Einstein,
and Cary Grant.
~ Peggy Lee

Our Thoughts:

Take your lessons wherever you find them. Even a pet can teach
you much about life. Don't filter the source of these lessons
through your biases—sometimes you can even learn from your
soon-to-be-ex.

Your Thoughts:

Am I open to all sources of learning?

❀

A man cannot jump over
his own shadow.
~ Yiddish Proverb

Our Thoughts:

Some things in life are simply not possible. We can't jump over
our own shadows, we can't change the past and very rarely can we
affect the future in any way that we can predict. All we have is
the flow of the "now," the present. Don't mull over what coulda
shoulda been. Pay attention to your life today.

Your Thoughts:

What is my life today?

❧

What you resist, persists.
~ Werner Erhard

Our Thoughts:
If you have a sink full of dirty dishes and you resist washing
them, they don't go away. If you resist washing them over a
long period of time, they become a real problem...odors, bugs,
health hazards. Deal with it.

Your Thoughts:
What am I resisting in my life?

❧

Sports learned in childhood
can be great energizers.
~ Venus Veritas

Our Thoughts:

How long has it been since you pedaled your way through the
neighborhood or skated around the rink?   Whether you roll
along on two wheels or four, you can recapture that wind-in-the-
face freedom you felt as a child. Try it!

Your Thoughts:

What childhood activities can I incorporate into my new life?

It is not easy to find happiness in ourselves,
and it is not possible to find it elsewhere.
~ Agnes Repplier

Our Thoughts:

If you look for happiness from outside yourself, you'll be doomed
to eternal disappointment. Happiness is self-generated, and though
difficult to achieve, it's the only ball game in town.

Your Thoughts:

Where is my happiness?

❂

I base my fashion taste on
what doesn't itch.
~ Gilda Radner

Our Thoughts:
Ruthlessly analyze your wardrobe. After all, you're a whole
new person now, and you deserve to look fresh and alive! Dig
out the old boring, worn, ill-fitting, or just plain ugly clothes
from your closet and drawers, pile them neatly in cartons and
donate them to charity. Somebody can still get a lot of good use
out of those clothes, and it doesn't have to be you.

Your Thoughts:
What items in my closet make me feel terrific?

❧

> We are all here on earth to help others;
> what on earth the others are here for I don't know.
> ~ W. H. Auden

Our Thoughts:

Our hearts feel pleasantly fuller when we incorporate kindness into our everyday interactions with other creatures. Grant the unasked-for favor. Speak aloud the compliment you just thought about your companion. Feed the birds. Thoughtfulness can become a habit.

Your Thoughts:

What random acts of kindness can I make a part of my life?

☯

To sit at the forest's edge sketching the bold wildflowers
In scarlets and mauves, defining the wood fern
In lacy, soft greens, will both honor nature
And grant you her peace.
~ Linda C. Senn

Our Thoughts:

No matter what your level of artistic talent, nature sketching can be fun. You might enjoy taking a sketch pad, a handful of colored pencils, and a folding chair to a park. Often you have to go no farther than the edge of the parking lot to have glorious, blooming "models" for your drawing delight. It has a curious way of opening your heart and spirit to the sun.

Your Thoughts:

Where shall I look for my "models"?

The very cave you are afraid to enter
turns out to be the source of what you are looking for.
~ Joseph Campbell

Our Thoughts:

Perhaps the cavern you're afraid to enter is single life itself. Or it may be the dating scene, or being completely responsible for the house repairs, or remembering the kids' birthdays. Divorcing takes a great deal of courage. There are so many caves and we can get so weary of confronting all those dragons. Those very caves can lead to unexpected treasure, and each of your new day-to-day adventures will be a step up the ladder of your personal growth.

Your Thoughts:

What areas am I afraid to explore?

Love, the quest; marriage, the conquest;
divorce, the inquest.
~ Helen Rowland

Our Thoughts:

While this may bring a wry smile to your lips, there is an inherent truth contained in this thought: inquests bring facts and truths to light. As miserable (or happy) as you may be during this period, take some time to review your marriage and come to some understanding of what you learned from it. Review, but don't get stuck in the past. If you haven't learned anything from being with your spouse, you haven't been paying attention.

Your Thoughts:

What have I learned from this marriage?

A room without books
is like a body without a soul.
~ Cicero

Our Thoughts:

Since you're reading this book right now, you probably like to read. The written word can be a solace and an escape from life's problems. Surround yourself with books and feed your soul.

Your Thoughts:

Which books comfort me now?

❦

One is not born a woman,
one becomes one.
~ Simone deBeauvoir

Our Thoughts:

The same can be said about becoming a man. Just being born doesn't give you a worthy personality or character. Divorce is an *event* in your very human life. It is not who you are.

Your Thoughts:

What does being a woman or a man mean to me?

Age doesn't matter unless you are a cheese.
~ Billie Burke

Our Thoughts:

Emerging from a divorce is an aging process…everyone feels old by the time it's over. If you happen also to be chronologically older, you may feel like Methuselah—ugly and unlovable. Give yourself some time. Find something that makes you feel young again. If you don't know what that would be, ask friends for suggestions.

Your Thoughts:

How do I feel about my chronological age? My emotional age?

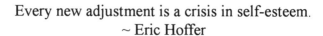

Every new adjustment is a crisis in self-esteem.
~ Eric Hoffer

Our Thoughts:

Poor self-esteem can churn up lots of nasty, internal dialogue. "I'm such a schlep... why can't I be smarter, funnier, richer...I fall up stairs, slop my coffee, I'm such a loser." Instead of wasting energy with this self-flagellation, focus on some positive aspect of yourself each day. A "Good For Me" notebook is a great place to jot down each day's discoveries. Little ones count as much as big ones. Explore the whole range from the pleasant chat you had with the grocery checker to the corporate deal you just closed. Learn to focus on the good. The more you search, the more you'll find.

Your Thoughts:

How shall I start my "good for me" notebook?

If we'd only stop trying to be happy
we'd have a pretty good time.
~ Edith Wharton

Our Thoughts:

The pursuit of happiness often brings just that...pursuit, not
happiness. Try living in the moment, enjoying what is, not what
you'd like it to be. Try on satisfaction instead of happiness and
see what happens.

Your Thoughts:

Am I living now, or am I pursuing?

Life is just a bowl of pits.
~ Rodney Dangerfield

Our Thoughts:

An effective pathway out of that bowl is to focus your attention on someone besides yourself. Plan a party for a friend, either a birthday or an unbirthday party, a bagel breaking, a wiener roast, or a garden party. The theme isn't important, as long as you're plotting to bring a smile to someone else's heart.

Your Thoughts:

Whose heart can I bring a smile to and how will I do it?

One doesn't discover new lands
without consenting to lose sight of the shore
for a very long time.
~ Andre Gide

Our Thoughts:

It's time to go swimming, sailing, yachting ... and time to lose
sight of the shore. You're already out there, after all. Divorce
does that. One minute you're in familiar married land, the next
you're in a strange territory. Just remember – the new lands
you'll discover hold the potential for growth and pleasure, even
if this divorce feels devastating. If you focus on the pain and
not the growth, your life won't be a pleasure to live.

Your Thoughts:

Where is my focus?

❂

Mysticism is, in essence, little more than a
certain intensity and depth of feeling
in regard to what is believed about the universe.
~ Bertrand Russell

Our Thoughts:

When everything in the world is turned upside down, as so often
happens during a divorce, belief systems come under scrutiny and
even under fire. Take some time to consider what you believe in.
Review your beliefs. Do they still work for you? If so, reaffirm
them. If not, look for what does work for you.

Your Thoughts:

What are my values today?

In each human heart are a tiger, a pig, an ass and a nightingale.
Diversity of character is due to their unequal activity.
~ Ambrose Bierce

Our Thoughts:

At first reading that sounds pretty unflattering, but the truth is we
could add a few more critters of our own – hound dog, chicken,
hyena, toad, louse – and so forth. And there's nothing inherently
"bad" about any one of these, as long as that aspect of us is kept
in balance with the rest. Even the mighty tiger-persona shouldn't
overshadow our gentler strengths. Balance of self is always a
worthy goal.

Your Thoughts:

What are some of my own animal characteristics?

❂

When people are bored, it is primarily
with their own selves.
~ Eric Hoffer

Our Thoughts:

It's almost cliché that by the sad end of a marriage both partners
feel like boring, useless, relatively ugly sacks of garbage. The
good news is – you won't feel that way forever! The other good
news is – the rediscovery of the interesting parts of you is in your
own hands. The process will be gradual but steady if you use
affirmations like "I'm an exciting human being, and I nurture my
good points and create new ones daily." Adopt this mantra or
one like it and repeat it often.

Your Thoughts:

How will I word my affirmation(s)?

I turned down a date once because I was looking for
someone a little closer to the top of the food chain.
~ Judy Tenuta

Our Thoughts:

Who, me? Get back in the dating scene? You've gotta be crazy!
Well, guess what ... most of those other single folks are just as
uncertain as you are.   One way to boost your conversation
quotient is to read the newspaper and news magazines, or if
you're TV oriented, watch the TV news magazines, and check
your computer for cutting edge news. They will keep you know-
ledgeable and conversant on a wealth of topics.

Your Thoughts:

Which avenues of information will I use to pep up my
conversation?

☯

Don't compromise yourself.
You are all you've got.
~ Janis Joplin

Our Thoughts:

Find your center. That place within you where you draw the line
and say to the world or anyone trying to intrude upon your boun-
daries "this far, no further". Don't give in. Don't give up. And
don't do anything you know to be wrong.

Your Thoughts:

Am I in touch with my center?

☯

Wine gives great pleasure, and
every pleasure is of itself good.
~ Samuel Johnson

Our Thoughts:

Suddenly you're being invited to house parties and dinners as a single. Accept with a smile, and show a touch of class by bringing a "thank you" bottle of wine for the host and hostess. It's fairly economical – easily under $10 – and is usually appropriate.

Your Thoughts:

What other small gift of thanks could I take to my host or hostess?

☯

Everything is funny as long
as it is happening to somebody else.
~ Will Rogers

Our Thoughts:

In the process of redefining who we are, there's a fierce tendency
toward earnestness, to take all that we do and say w-a-y too
seriously. Remember to chuckle at your own goofs and foibles.
Everyone has them, but we have a better shot at keeping them in
perspective when we view them with a wry sense of humor.

Your Thoughts:

When was the last time I screwed up and was able to
spontaneously laugh about it?

❧

Our entire life, with our fine moral code and
our precious freedom, consists ultimately
in accepting ourselves as we are.
~ Jean Anouilh

Our Thoughts:

Before accepting yourself as you are, you have to know who and
how you are. Take some time to rediscover yourself.

Your Thoughts:

What do I want? What do I like? What are my goals? Where am
I headed?

◉

Mentoring enriches the soul.
~ Venus Veritas

Our Thoughts:

What of your various areas of expertise could you pass along to a
protégé? The act of mentoring can create lasting growth and
knowledge as well as a special kind of bonding. For those going
through a major life transition, it affirms their level of knowing and
transforms giving into sharing.

Your Thoughts:

Where and how could I mentor someone?

❂

Women must try to do things as men have tried.
When they fail, their failure must be
but a challenge to others.
~ Amelia Earhart, in her last letter to
her husband

Our Thoughts:

Sometimes women (and men, too) are afraid to try to do *anything*
because of the possibility of failure, rejection or a host of other
reasons. Be courageous! Bring your fear along for the ride, but
don't let it keep you off of it! No matter what your concerns ...
you can do it!

Your Thoughts:

What scares me?

❂

Poetry is fact given over to imagery.
~ Rod McKuen

Our Thoughts:

Have you tried your hand at writing poetry lately? If not, why not? You could write in metered, rhyming verse, or modern, free style, or in one of the traditional forms like haiku or cinquain. Just observe the world around you – nature, humanity, folly – and begin jotting down words. Play with them. And don't worry about whether anyone else on this earth would like your verses or not. They're all yours.

Your Thoughts:

How do I feel about writing poetry?

☯

Does taking a risk *mean* you're healthy, or
does it *make* you healthy?
~ Venus Veritas

Our Thoughts:

If there's nobody out there criticizing you, you're probably not trying hard enough. It's not that we yearn for criticism, but to encounter none may mean that we aren't taking any chances at all, either in thought or action. To be fully alive means to take risks, however minor they may seem to someone else.

Your Thoughts:

What small risks can I begin taking in my life?

❧

A correspondence course of passion was,
for her, the perfect and ideal
relationship with a man.
~ Aldous Huxley

Our Thoughts:

Those of you whose social energies lag behind your libido in the recovery period can do some great practice flirting over the Internet singles' sites. And, yes, the opportunities for cybersex (erotic online correspondence) abound. It's the ultimate in safe sex, and might be the temporary outlet you're looking for. Or you can connect with someone who prefers the more traditional online-poetry-and-flowers routine to restart your flirtation engine.

Your Thoughts:

How will I describe myself to an online friend?

❂

I shut my eyes in order to see.
~ Paul Gauguin

Our Thoughts:

This is a time to go within, to be still. Close your eyes. Take a deep breath. Quiet your mind and shut off that incessant voice in the back of your head that's always judging. Be with yourself long enough to see what's necessary in your life.

Your Thoughts:

What can I do to become quiet within?

❂

You may be disappointed if you fail,
but you are doomed if you don't try.
~ Beverly Sills

Our Thoughts:

This famous opera star has had an illustrious career, but she surely wouldn't have attained such heights if she never tried new things. When she retired from singing, she went on to become the General Director and President of the New York City Opera. That job was outside her previous experience, but she was willing to try. Now she has a whole new career. Try. Do.

Your Thoughts:

How easy or difficult is it for me to try something new?

☯

I will always cherish the initial misconceptions
I had about you.
~ Unknown

Our Thoughts:

Yes, when you first met your now ex, he or she was undoubtedly
Ms. or Mr. Utterly Perfect. But it didn't work out. You're
starting separate lives now. So whatever musty illusions you still
cling to, get over them and move on. It's almost impossible to
reach for the future while you're still hanging on to the past.

Your Thoughts:

How am I still clinging to my old misconceptions of my ex?

❧

The scars that form over the wounds of our lives
leave us stronger than before.
~ Venus Veritas

Our Thoughts:

After all the arguing and negotiating are concluded, and the
divorce has been granted, the wounds will heal. And the invisible
scars that remain will make you a stronger and a more resilient
person than before – honest.

Your Thoughts:

In what ways am I already feeling stronger than before?

❂

Nostalgia isn't what it used to be.
~ Anonymous

Our Thoughts:
Living in the past can become an albatross around your neck.
Those times were seldom as rosy as you see them in hindsight,
and will do little toward you living a fuller life today.

Your Thoughts:
In what way do I still tend to live in the past?

◉

A joyful and delicious life is best achieved by paying
equal attention to your body, mind, and spirit.
~ Venus Veritas

Our Thoughts:

To avoid the temptation of immersing yourself in just one of these
three elemental aspects of yourself, try writing all of your activities
on a large calendar using a different colored highlighter to mark
body, mind, or spirit. You can then tell at a glance if all your plans
are centered around one to the detriment of the other two.

Your Thoughts:

How can I achieve balance in body, mind, and spirit in my weekly
activities?

❡

I have so little sex appeal that my
gynecologist calls me "sir."
~ Joan Rivers

Our Thoughts:

Divorce can leave your self-esteem in tatters, but don't look to others to validate your sexuality. Honor yourself by keeping up an attractive, healthy appearance, using a bit of cologne or after shave, keeping your hair in stylish trim, and whatever else it takes so that you'll respect your *own* sexuality.

Your Thoughts:

What small props and activities make me feel good about my sexual identity?

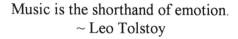

Music is the shorthand of emotion.
~ Leo Tolstoy

Our Thoughts:

It's been said that music can soothe the savage breast, but did you know it can also smooth the savage transition? This is a great time to explore different areas of music, and perhaps discover a new style. Listen to the radio, check out free, live music at book store cafes and coffee houses, scan the entertainment section of your paper, and swap CD's with friends. Close your eyes, and immerse yourself in the sweet sounds.

Your Thoughts:

What are *my* music preferences?

Be yourself. Who else is better qualified?
~ Frank J. Giblin II

Our Thoughts:

Divorce and starting over gives us a glorious opportunity to
finally be ourselves without twisting our persona to conform to
the Other's expectations. Explore your own passions and peeves,
your joys and goals just as you would with a new friend.

Your Thoughts:

What are some of my passions in life?

☯

When a man is wrapped up in himself,
he makes a pretty small package.
~ John Ruskin

Our Thoughts:

Directing your sympathies outward can be very refreshing at a
time like this. Try volunteering for a few hours a week (or
month) at a nearby hospital, school, charity, or other place in
your community. Although it may be a struggle to overcome
your emotional lassitude, the time devoted to helping others will
actually leave you feeling like a "good person" – a reality we
can come to doubt on the rocky path through divorce.

Your Thoughts:

Where can I ask about volunteering a few hours a month?

❦

Contraceptives should be used on every conceivable occasion.
~ From *The Last Goon Show of All*

Our Thoughts:

When you feel you're ready for real, live, interactive sex again, stock up on condoms. We're *all* susceptible to sexually transmitted diseases. In fact one of the fastest growing segments of the population to test positive for HIV is middle age females. No one is immune. Practice safe sex.

Your Thoughts:

Which store can I go to where I will feel less self-conscious buying a box of condoms?

❦

When you know and respect your own Inner Nature,
you know where you belong.
~ Benjamin Hoff in *The Tao of Pooh*

Our Thoughts:

In a moribund marriage, we tend to shape ourselves to fit the comfort of our spouse just to keep the peace. Somewhere through the years, we may very nearly forget who we are under the accommodating façade. Vow right now never, ever to lose yourself again in order to please another. The process of becoming single again allows you to rediscover your own inner nature. Treasure and honor it when you do.

Your Thoughts:

What false roles did I play in my marriage just to accommodate the Other?

☯

The will to disbelieve is
the strongest deterrent to wider horizons.
~ Hans Holzer

Our Thoughts:

Our world has reached a point in its spiritual development when
such learned scholars as Elisabeth Kubler-Ross and Brian L.
Weiss, M.D. are writing about life after death and relating their
own experiences of the spirit. If you haven't explored other
theories and teachings beyond those you grew up with, now is a
great time to do so. Ask your librarian or book store clerk to
direct you to the New Age, metaphysical, philosophy or religion
section, and give your curiosity full rein.

Your Thoughts:

What religious and philosophical areas do I want to learn more
about?

☯

I don't think of myself as single.
I'm romantically challenged.
~ Stephanie H. Piro

Our Thoughts:

Making fun of icons and institutionalized concepts is fun, and
that's precisely what you should be having... fun! Put your
tongue firmly in your cheek and make jokes about your status –
it's a way both to relieve your own tension and to become better
acquainted with your new identity as a single person.

Your Thoughts:

Where can I find the humor in life?

❂

If you think you can, you can.
And if you think you can't, you're right.
~ Mary Kay Ash

Our Thoughts:
This woman founded Mary Kay Cosmetics. She is living proof
that starting with nothing and making it into something is possible.
She thought she could. She was right.

Your Thoughts:
Do I think I can?

❧

What a wonderful life I've had!
I only wish I'd realized it sooner.
~ Colette

Our Thoughts:

You're having a terrific life. Yes! Right now, this minute. It's the only one you have and the only time you can have it. Be fully present. Be in your "now." Experience your wonderful life as you're having it, not later in your memory.

Your Thoughts:

What are the good things about my life now?

Congratulations ... by the time you finish this book, you will have done a lot of soul-searching and set your feet firmly on the road to positive new beginnings.

We wish you a happy journey, for personal growth never ends – it's an exciting, ongoing adventure.

Good luck and Godspeed!

Linda, Mary and, of course, Venus Veritas

Bibliography

Like so many authors before us, we've spent not years, but *decades* collecting quotations and witty sayings from magazines, books, friends, radio and television. Many of our favorites appear in many different resources. However we do want to express our thanks to the following books for being such amazing quotation treasure troves:

... Robert Byrne's wonderful 637 Best Things Anybody Ever Said series from Fawcett Crest.
... "The Concise Oxford Dictionary of Quotations" second edition, Oxford University Press.
... "Barnes & Noble Book of Quotations" edited by Robert I. Fitzhenry, Barnes & Noble Books, Division of Harper & Row.
... "Peter's Quotations: Ideas for Our Time" by Laurence J. Peter, Bantam Books.
... "Believing in Ourselves: The Wisdom of Women" Ariel Book/ Andrews and McMeel.

Herbert, Frank, *Children of Dune*, New York: Berkley Books, 1976.
Hoff, Benjamin *The Tao of Pooh,* New York: Penguin Books, 1982.
Kopp, Sheldon, *No Hidden Meanings, An Illustrated Eschatological Laundry List*, Palo Alto, CA: Science and Behavior Books, 1975.
Osbon, Diane, edited by. *Reflections on the Art of Living: A Joseph Campbell Companion,* New York: HarperCollins, 1991.

... and all the great magazines that offer pearls of wisdom through other people's words.

∾ ∾ ∾

About the authors ...

Linda C. Senn was born (and stayed) in St. Louis, Missouri, and now enjoys life in Kirkwood, an historic suburb, a few blocks from the Unitarian church in which she is actively involved.

Her children, Heather and Kevin, are the touchstones of her heart.

After working in various areas of business, from estimating to new department set-ups, Linda turned to her first love – writing, and for the past ten years her articles and accompanying photos have appeared in magazines and newspapers across the country.

She also wrote "Your Pocket Divorce Guide" and "10 Effective Ways to Promote Your Seminar," and is at work on the upcoming "Midlife Recovery Journal" with writing partner Mary Stuart.

In addition to writing and publishing, Linda presents seminars on preparing for divorce, making a fresh start thereafter, developing your creativity, and promoting your small business.

Mary Stuart brings a wealth of information to the subject of divorce. She holds degrees in psychology and counseling and has seen the pain and devastation of divorce from both a clinical and personal perspective.

As a result of the second divorce and the ensuing sea change, she joined Pen Central Communications to offer her expertise in writing and seminar presentation. Under the aegis of GGSeminars, she and her co-author created "Preparing for Divorce," a workshop for men and women who are experiencing the first pangs of separation. It's concise and filled with information and support. She has lived in various locales around the country, and currently lives in St. Louis with a contemplated move to Phoenix. She is enjoying her new careers as an author, trainer and personal coach.

Linda and Mary, and their alter ego Venus Veritas, would enjoy hearing your comments on this book, on your divorce experience and on life in general! Your can write to them c/o Pen Central Press, P. O. Box 220369, St. Louis MO 63122.

Index

-A-

Acceptance, 221
Adaptability, 72
Adversaries, 166
Adversity, 150
Advice, 22, 23, 109
Affirmations, 27, 130, 216
Age, 209
Aggressive, 41
Alcohol, 163
Alone, 52, 62, 126, 180
Anger, 40, 65, 100, 104, 120, 128
Anticipation, 151
Anxiety, 95
Approval, 184
Arguing, 71
Art, 204
Assertiveness, 41, 155
Attitude, 170
Attorneys, 73, 169

-B-

Balance, 106, 215, 231
Beliefs, 93, 214
Blame, 185
Boredom, 216

-C-

Challenge, 66
Change, 37, 61, 72, 76, 79, 108, 125, 145, 146, 159, 179
Children, 56
Clothes, 202
Comfort, 207
Compassion, 122
Compromise, 155, 218
Confidence, 237
Consistency, 187
Control, 24, 98
Counseling, 82, 113
Courage, 42, 53, 58, 66, 80, 146, 205
Crazy, 17, 31

-D-

Dating, 137, 167, 186, 192, 217
Depression, 95, 136, 161
Diplomacy, 118, 124
Dreams, 183

-E-

Eating, 32, 64

-L-

Laughter, 55, 84, 88, 115, 119, 136, 140, 181, 220
Learning, 197, 206
Legal, 73
Lethargy, 15
Lonely, 20, 62

-M-

Malice, 139
Meditation, 135
Mentoring, 222
Mistakes, 26, 51, 82, 123, 178
Morale, 77, 86, 87
Music, 234

-N-

Nature, 190
Negativity, 57, 115
Nostalgia, 232

-O-

Obstacles, 143

-P-

Past, 83
Patience, 78, 168
Perfection, 51

Perspective, 54
Planning, 24, 43, 94, 98, 121, 141
Play, 121
Poetry, 224
Present, 63, 99, 103, 114,198, 242
Problem solving, 131, 189

-R-

Reality, 54, 75, 92, 151, 194
Reason, 47
Resiiience, 30
Resistance, 199
Restlessness, 182
Risk, 213, 225, 228
Romance, 29, 74, 107, 114, 167

-S-

Sanity, 178
Satisfaction, 211
Self-esteem, 74, 76, 77, 111, 139, 154, 210, 221, 233
Self-examination, 45, 227, 235, 239
Senses, 117, 190
Settlement, 96
Sex, 29, 147, 226, 233, 238
Simplify, 81
Sleep, 115, 140, 148

Order these Pen Central books:

"The Divorce Recovery Journal" ... $15.95
　　by Linda C. Senn and Mary Stuart, M.A.
　　　　Shipping & Handling $3.00 per book
　　　　(MO residents add $1.16 tax per book)
　　　　ISBN 0-9665672-2-6 (256 pg.)

"Your Pocket Divorce Guide" ... $13.95
　　by Linda C. Senn
　　　　Shipping & Handling $2.50 per book
　　　　(MO residents add $1.01 tax per book)
　　　　ISBN 0-9665672-1-8 (96 pg.)

"10 Effective Ways to Promote Your Seminar" ... $9.95
　　by Linda C. Senn
　　　　Shipping & Handling $2.00 per book
　　　　(MO residents add $.72 tax per book)
　　　　ISBN 0-9665672-0-X (48 pg.)

Books are sent by First Class mail.

Make checks payable to **Pen Central** and mail with your order to:

Pen Central Press
Order Department
P. O. Box 220369
St. Louis MO 63122-0369

PEN
CENTRAL
PRESS